MOTIVATION AND EMOTION

Motivation and Emotion

PHIL EVANS

ROUTLEDGE
London and New York

First published in 1989
by Routledge
11 New Fetter Lane, London EC4P 4EE
29 West 35th Street, New York, NY 10001

© 1989 Phil Evans

Phototypeset in 10pt Times by
Mews Photosetting, Beckenham, Kent

Printed in Great Britain by
Billing & Sons Ltd, Worcester

All rights reserved. No part of this book may be reprinted or
reproduced or utilized in any form or by any electronic, mechanical, or
other means, now known or hereafter invented, including photocopying
and recording, or in any information storage or retrieval system, without
permission in writing from the publishers.

British Library Cataloguing in Publication Data

Evans, Phil
    Motivation and emotion.
    1. Man. Motivation
    I. Title
    153.8

    ISBN 0-415-01475-1
    ISBN 0-415-01476-X (pbk.)

Library of Congress Cataloging in Publication Data

Evans, Phil.
    Motivation and emotion.

    Bibliography: p.
    Includes index.
    1. Motivation (Psychology) 2. Emotions. I. Title.
BF503.E94   1988   153.8   88-26356
ISBN 0-415-01475-1
ISBN 0-415-01476-X (pbk.)

Contents

Figures and tables

Preface

Whether to write a book and how to approach the endeavour are both questions which authors usually address with some ambivalence. The brief in this case seemed reasonably straightforward: a book which could serve as a text for undergraduate courses in Motivation and Emotion, which would be somewhat more than a basic introduction (the aim of my previous book in the Methuen *Essential Psychology* series) but be short enough to be priced so as to appeal to the much stretched pockets of contemporary students. Straightforward the brief may have been, but realizable? That clearly must be left for readers to determine themselves.

Although the book is primarily meant for psychology undergraduates, I hope it may also evoke some interest in the results of psychological research among a more 'lay' readership. There has had to be some compromise: terms which I expect a first year psychology student to have encountered in introductory reading are sometimes used without explanation; however I believe that on the whole the book may prove accessible to a somewhat wider readership than simply students.

Ambivalence also arises with regard to content. The areas of motivation and emotion are such huge fields that any author who produces anything which is called a 'text' must accept with resignation that certain readers will question the organization and content whatever it be. In a book of this length some sins of omission will no doubt be starkly evident. I only hope that 'expert' readers, should there be such, will each point to different lacunae, thereby at least demonstrating the impossibility of pleasing all.,

Selection and organization of content, however, is not just a cold rational process of best guessing. This book would never have been written had not the author wanted to write it for more personal reasons: in short, to bring together his own thoughts and perspectives on a wider area of psychology stretching out beyond his immediate focus of research. With this in view, both in style and argument, I have not attempted to disguise bias (and perhaps even prejudice) in the way that I have discussed the topics and concerns of the following chapters. The end product, I believe, is best seen as a book that can serve as a text and reference source, rather than a written-to-formula textbook.

One final point on content. There is a companion volume which could be written on motivation and emotion. It would deal with what are sometimes called 'higher' motives and feelings.The reader will not find in this volume a discussion of spirituality or even some of the meanings given to the word 'love'. Religious yearning and the experience of existential *Angst* get a sideways glance in the first chapter but my final decision has been to write a certain kind of book which reasonably fits the title but not to write in any sense *the* book. The very importance of the omitted issues in a sense argues for their own exclusion on the grounds that they should not be diluted in a thin soup into which everything is thrown.

The structure of the book means that certain traditional topics in motivation, while not being totally excluded, are sometimes mentioned in conjunction with other issues and do not get the usual textbook title or sub-title. Examples are conformity and need for approval — important social motives to be sure — which raise their heads both in the discussion of aggression in chapter 5 and in the discussion of general goal-seeking behaviour in chapter 9. For some topics, then, the reader might wish to refer to the index pages rather than the Contents page. The treatment of such issues may lack substance, having no traditional textbook elaboration and no classic reference list. So be it. Any structure facilitates and inhibits in equal measure.

Finally, although each chapter ends with a brief conclusion which tries to summarize the perspective of the chapter, I have stopped short of recommending specific further reading. This would be too uneven a task across the different chapters. Certain of the references in the final bibliography, however, the student may feel it appropriate to follow up: fairly recent review articles or books.

Acknowledgements

These are many. I must thank, if not list, several colleagues in various groves of academe, and particularly in my home department at NELP, who have discussed issues, led me to certain references, commented on bits of manuscript draft, and collectively offered me the academic support necessary to finish the book. Errors remain mine for the claiming.

I owe a great debt to the many undergraduates at NELP who have given me feedback on the lecture courses that have developed in tandem with the writing of the book. Two persons should be singled out for special mention: Nigel Haunch, who has diligently acted as reader and first stage proof-reader; finally, Mary Ann Kernan of Routledge has provided excellent encouragement throughout the project.

Phil Evans
London, 1987

1

Introduction and overview

The area of motivation and emotion in psychology is potentially vast and has ill-defined boundaries. In order to highlight just what are the central concerns of the area, we might care to imagine the free associations an ordinary person is likely to give to the two key words of this book's title. Probable associations would be along the lines: 'passions', 'urges', 'instincts', 'goals', 'rewards', 'carrots', 'sticks', and so on. In other words, and more prosaically, motivation is about specifying the reasons why an organism is, at any particular time, behaving in the way that it is. In this book, we shall principally, but not exclusively, be concerned with the human organism.

There is general acknowledgement in our culture that people do many of the things which they do because they find them pleasurable, and avoid many things because they find them painful. Such a theoretical position might be called 'guiding hedonism'. The area of emotion involves the delineation and investigation of those same hedonic experiential states. For that reason the areas of motivation and emotion are closely linked, and not surprisingly they share the same Latin root in the verb *movere*: to move. We are moved to do things, and we are moved by things.

A little conceptual analysis, at this stage, may set the ground for the issues which are addressed in the substantive chapters that follow. For much of the time we shall be asking why certain kinds of activity and feelings occur and the answers to those 'why' questions will be seen as explanations. It is fitting therefore to begin with a discussion of what we mean by the term explanation.

SCIENTIFIC EXPLANATION

The reasons that the man or woman in the street may give to 'explain' why someone is behaving in a certain way might not satisfy a behavioural scientist. The word 'explanation' in science suggests that we know what necessary and sufficient conditions need to obtain in order that a certain phenomenon should occur. In the physical sciences, such conditions can often be stated with a degree of exactitude, such that we can very accurately predict the phenomenon in question. Even the physical sciences, however, move towards what might be termed 'measured uncertainty' as they reach the dizzy heights of current theory. Psychological science reaches its uncertainty at the outset and for obvious reasons. A particular piece of behaviour is usually determined by so many factors that specifying all of them is impossible. Psychologists are not thereby prevented from scientific prediction. It simply becomes the case that their predictions are usually probabilistic. We predict that certain outcomes are more probable than others when certain conditions pertain. Psychological science is not any the lesser for being a probabilistic science (though not a few psychologists seem in a hurry to suggest that psychology is not a real science). The 'bottom line' is surely that any predictive statement should be testable with regard to its truth or falsehood. Certainly psychology as a discipline does evoke keen interest among philosophers of science and many would doubtless see it as more than just a probabilistic science. Without unduly widening the debate, most interested parties could at least agree that when a probabilistic statement is made it should be in principle as testable as any other statement about the empirical world.

EXPLANATION AND THE NEVER-ENDING

Providing an explanation is potentially an endless affair. It is so, in two kinds of way. The first is familiar to any parent with a child who has reached a certain age when 'why' questions become matters of great moment. If the cause of z is given as y the next question is what causes y; answer x, and so on. The really accomplished child performers can take us back through the alphabet at a rate of knots. What constitutes a 'proper' or 'full' explanation is not a hard or fast matter. We ourselves choose where to limit potentially endless causal chains, and we do so according to what seems appropriate in the context of our giving the explanation.

The second way in which explanation can be never-ending refers not to the potentially infinite length of a causal chain, but to potentially infinite levels of analysis that can be applied to any link in the chain. A person's action becomes the movement of an arm; the movement of an arm becomes the activity of nerves, and so on. This form of infinite regress is well known and is called 'reductionism'. Proper explanation is not here a question of where we choose to end, but where we choose to begin. A common reductionist fallacy is that 'explanation' somehow gets better as so-called 'molar' events are broken down into their 'molecular' constituents. In psychology, the worst manifestation of this fallacy is the mistaken belief that physiologically couched explanations are better than 'mere' psychological ones. Once again, the truth is that 'proper' explanation has to do with the context in which a question is asked and the kind of answer that is expected.

EXPLAINING AND UNDERSTANDING

Some, no doubt, would see a great deal of overlap in the use of these two concepts. After all, people often ask for an explanation of something in order to understand it. However, although scientific explanation entails a type of understanding, the opposite is not always true. People often content themselves with an understanding which falls short of scientific explanation. People are highly motivated to seek meaning in their lives, and so pervasive is such 'effort after meaning' that the scope of science is seen as extremely limited in terms of the questions it can answer. They therefore seek to 'understand' themselves and the world by other means: light-heartedly perhaps through tea-leaves and playing-cards; more seriously through systems of thought such as religions and schools of psychoanalysis.

There should really be no need for conflict between the search for explanation and the search for understanding. Often, however, there is an undeniable muddle. It would be wrong, for example, to confuse a psychoanalyst's 'interpretation' of a client's dream with a scientific explanation. As Rycroft (1966), himself a psychoanalyst, has pointed out, psychoanalysis does not seek explanation in any scientific fashion, as if it were some rival system to empirical psychology; rather it seeks to impose structure and meaning on what otherwise might be a chaotic tableau of an individual's experiences. Of course exercises in one discipline might provide insights for another, and most would agree that some interesting and empirically testable propositions might on occasion emerge from psychoanalytic theorizing.

The desire for meaning as a fundamental human motive has not

3

gone unrecognized by psychologists. Indeed it has been a theme, implicit or explicit, in the writings of most so-called humanistic psychologists. This particular book chooses to concentrate on less weighty motives than the need for meaning in an individual's existence. Human beings, aware as they are of their own mortality, do occupy much of their time in easier pursuits and their more everyday preoccupations are those that are more readily approached by the empirical method. It is recognized, however, that this limitation of coverage is imposed and is not a value judgement on what is omitted. If I had to admit to a prejudice, it would be that among those who could meaningfully call themselves 'existentialist' thinkers, I find communication of issues more vivid and straightforward among philosophers, novelists, and even theologians, than among the ranks of psychologists.

WHERE WE FIND EXPLANATIONS

Motivational words in common usage often suggest certain locations when explaining behaviour. Words such as 'instinct', 'urge', 'drive', 'impulse', 'intention' share that aspect of meaning that suggests looking inside an agent to discover the cause of an activity. These inward-looking motivational words can be further sub-divided into those which imply crude biological causation and those which mean something more refined. In the former category are those suggestive, to the lay person, of inborn tendencies to action, and, when they are used in respect of human behaviour, there is an implicit suggestion of motivation shared with other animals. These are the obvious implications of the way such words as 'instinct' and 'drive' are used in common parlance. On the other hand, a word such as 'intention' suggests to the lay mind something in the nature of a mental cause. The ordinary person would follow Descartes in assuming a dualism of mind and body, mental and physical. When such a thing as 'intention' is attributed to cats and dogs and other favoured infra-humans it is often a sign that their status is being raised to that of mind-owners.

Not all our motivational words point inward. Words like 'reward', 'goal', 'incentive', 'penalty' refer to things out there in the environment, things which most societies hope will exercise some motivational control over individuals. Whether we tend on the whole to find our explanations for behaviour inside or outside, in mental or in physical terms, tends to reflect the image of humanity to which we are ideologically committed. An inclination to use inner words and mind words suggests a view which stresses the importance of individuality and free will. A tendency to use inner and body words suggests a pessimistic view of people as the inevitable victim of blind motives which will inevitably be expressed. 'That's human nature' is the favourite cliché of this ideological clique. The use of outer words suggests on the one hand an optimistic view of humanity as capable of great achievements if the right environment is provided, but also a pessimistic one in the sense that individuals are not really free agents — they simply react according to environmental contingencies.

Although psychologists might wish to present themselves as ideologically neutral scientists, the fact is that motivational words from ordinary language are used in their theories and do keep their full implications. Behaviourally inclined theorists, in so far as they stress outer determinants of behaviour, are sometimes seen as reducing humanity to responding automata; psychoanalysts, with their talk of instinctual impulses, reduce us to a collection of blindly driven psychic apparatuses, while cognitivists provide the ultimate in boredom by reducing us to information processors. Such criticisms would be valid if theoreticians were blinkered enough to believe that their models of man and woman were any more than working models. The truth is that the free-will versus determinism debate is not a genuine one, in the sense that there are not arguments for one side or against the other. As individuals in our everyday lives we assume we have free will, and we attribute it to others. A behavioural scientist, on the other hand, can only proceed usefully by assuming as a working hypothesis that behaviour is determined. Fortunately behavioural scientists usually have a clear sense of when they are on and when they are off duty, and for the most part have robust defences against trying to predict their own behaviour — something which otherwise could lead to logical problems.

We come now to an overview of subsequent chapters of this book. In these chapters, all of the causal locations mentioned will be emphasized at different points. This is not to be taken as flabby eclecticism, rather as an assertion that all the 'models of humanity' so far referred to are necessary for a proper appreciation of the behaviours which we seek to understand. To illuminate certain aspects of behaviour, we shall consider human beings as biological organisms, which they are. To illuminate others, we shall see humans and other animals as behaviour-emitters under the control of environmental stimuli, which to a demonstrable degree we and other animals are. Finally, we shall give equal consideration to human beings as autonomous agents, acting on their environments, receiving input, retrieving memories, making decisions, and executing responses: all things that we undoubtedly do. In some chapters all these views of humanity will share the stage; in others one view will tend to dominate. At the end of the book, it is hoped the reader will have a rounded appreciation of what makes people tick — an idiomatic phrase that is yet to be bettered as a description of what most non-psychologists would consider to be the psychologist's area of expertise.

OVERVIEW OF SUBSEQUENT CHAPTERS

The next four chapters of the book comprise a section which is titled 'Biological imperatives?' and each offers a succinct review of research on motivational factors in regard to a specific activity: eating, sleeping, sexual, and aggressive activity. All these activities have an important role for biological factors in their determination. They are activities indulged in by other animals as well as human beings. Eating we know ultimately satisfies a survival need. Sleeping, although we are less clear about its relation to survival, is certainly a behaviour which, like eating, becomes intensely craved when deprivation is experienced. Sexual activity is certainly necessary for the survival of the species, and the survival of genes. Aggression is also to differing degrees the expression of a behavioural repertoire which many species have evolved presumably because it has some survival value.

We have however deliberately put a question mark after the title 'Biological imperatives'. Why? In the end, the task of this book in regard to motivation is to explain why *activities* are engaged in, and, while the stark term 'hunger', for example, might be taken as referring to an exclusively biological motive, the activity of *eating* is determined by factors additional to those stemming from physiological need. The same argument applies to the other so-called biological imperatives.

The sixth chapter maintains an interest in things physiological but addresses the area of emotion, as well as the area of so-called 'emergency' motivation derived from the body's primitive responses to threat. We often talk of 'gut emotion'; in this chapter we ask to what extent is feedback from 'gut reactions' a necessary component of emotional feeling. How much does our body tell us about what we are feeling, and how much is due to the brain's cool assessment of the sort of situation we are in?

The seventh chapter moves towards those activities which, though they may be rooted in matters of survival, take on some complexity in the case of human beings. Those activities are 'predicting' and 'controlling' what happens in the environment. We begin this important chapter by placing such activities in a firm comparative (i.e. across-species) context. Only after doing this, do we look at some of the special ways in which humans differ from other animals in their motivation to cope with the uncertainties of life.

The eighth chapter assesses the historical and current status of those very influential theories of motivation which point to behaviour generally being energized by a hypothetical force, such as drive or arousal. This chapter highlights some of the difficulties of trying prematurely to marry quasi-physiological concepts and behavioural ones, and suggests how cognitive 'information-processing' models may be capable of providing better predictions of efficiency in the performance of tasks.

In the second part of this chapter we skirt the area of emotion again and address the issue of 'felt' arousal. We explore individual differences in the degree to which people seek high arousal states, thrills, and excitement. We also explore why all of us seem to see low arousal sometimes as unpleasant (boredom) and sometimes pleasant (relaxation); equally, sometimes we see high arousal as unpleasant (anxiety) and sometimes pleasant (excitement).

In chapter 9 we could be said to develop further some of the 'mastery' motifs implicit in chapter 7. Here we are more concerned however with long-term mastery in the form of achievement. We ask why some people, in a variety of areas where success and failure are salient outcomes, go on trying and persisting while others give up or do not get involved in the first place. In some ways, this chapter covers the sort of research which many will see as lying at the heart of motivation. We shall see that with regard to the pursuit of goals, many competing motives — including social ones, such as 'to be liked and approved of' and 'to conform' — can get in the way of any simple need to achieve success.

The final chapter returns to the area of emotion and explores further the role of cognition in relation to emotion. We try to disentangle definitional confusion and genuine differences of opinion. We utilize the broader term 'affect' in deference to those who see emotions as complex entities automatically involving cognitive appraisals of a situation. We provide a summary of an important 'affect' theory — opponent process theory — which seems to involve little in the way of cognitive involvement. We also finally look at the way that affect can cue cognitions and vice versa.

2

Eating

THE CONCEPT OF HOMEOSTASIS

Our physical survival depends on a certain stability being maintained inside our bodies. The term 'homeostasis' is used to describe the regulatory processes that contribute to the maintenance of stability. A thermostat is a specific example of a 'homeostat'. It is activated by signals from an environment which initiate activity until such a time as different signals arrive and shut down the activity, thus initiating in turn an 'off-period' which will eventually prompt the return of the 'on-signals'. Thus homeostasis is not in reality about keeping an absolutely constant state; rather it is about keeping within a narrow bandwidth by the use of feedback controls. The essence of homeostasis is the negative feedback loop: an activity is initiated which results finally in signals which terminate that activity.

Many instances of homeostatic regulation are concerned with unconscious automatic processes. We are not, for example, usually conscious of our absolutely basic need for oxygen, and our breathing is not therefore usually spoken of as motivated behaviour, although the patient with severe emphysema may well exhibit 'motivated' struggling for breath and only too real awareness of need. The same principles apply to many other regulatory functions. We are not in the normal scheme of things much consciously involved in keeping our body temperatures in the close vicinity of 37 degrees Celsius, although much motivated behaviour can ensue in an English winter from the failure of central heating boilers. Thus homeostasis, in so far as it concerns the constant fulfilment of biological survival needs, occurs unconsciously and automatically except *in extremis*.

There are however survival needs which more directly have what we undoubtedly would term motivational significance. The textbook case, and one therefore we shall adopt, is the need for food. *In extremis*, hunger motivates eating, but eating is not otherwise an unconscious activity; indeed it is often the most attention-given of our daily activities. Ultimately biologically based, eating may be; simply biological, it decidedly is not. For that reason psychologists and physiologists have over many years been interested in mapping out the interplay of factors which do determine the eating behaviour of people and organisms in general.

MAINTAINING A CONSTANT BODY-WEIGHT

With the possible exception of first-world twentieth-century human beings, it is the case that organisms generally have finely tuned abilities to maintain a constant body-weight over long periods of time. This suggests sensitive homeostatic feedback mechanisms, which respond on the one hand to physiological evidence of depletion and on the other hand to signals of satiety. A study of normality in this regard may help to illuminate processes underlying abnormality. In human beings, eating disorders have been a flourishing area of research for some years, such disorders ranging from common or garden obesity to the more bizarre self-starving of anorexia nervosa and binge eating of bulimia. We shall consider these at a later stage. We begin with a consideration of how eating behaviour is normally regulated.

PERIPHERAL FACTORS

In the early years of this century the famous physiologist Walter Cannon put forward a theory of drinking and eating motivation which has sometimes aptly been called the 'spit and rumble' theory. This theory maintained the importance of peripheral cues in the control of eating and drinking. Thus a dry mouth will prompt drinking, while an empty rumbling stomach will initiate eating. In Cannon's view the motivational concept of hunger was synonymous with a collection of peripheral cues associated with a growing state of food depletion.

As a theory which addresses the necessary conditions for regulated eating, that is, the maintenance of a set bodyweight, peripheral theory cannot pass muster. Some fairly obvious findings contradict it. Patients who undergo complete gastrectomies do not lose the ability to regulate their eating, although they will adopt different eating habits that reflect the absence of a stomach. While it is possible to argue that other peripheral cues 'take over', it is not a plausible line of argument to chase some *sine qua non* of hunger motivation down the duodenum or other part of the viscera! If peripheral cues really were essential we would expect at least some disruption from removal of the entire stomach. Equally compelling evidence against the peripheral theory comes from early work which showed that severing the vagus nerve which connects stomach and brain does not prevent homeostasis being maintained.

To assert that peripheral cues are unnecessary for successful food-intake regulation is not to diminish their importance as governing factors in the eating behaviour of normal intact organisms. If however we wish to look for areas in which damage is genuinely associated with disruption of food-intake regulation then we must move away from the periphery and into the central nervous system.

CENTRAL NERVOUS SYSTEM MECHANISMS

Early on this century it was known that injury to the base of the brain in the vicinity of the hypothalamus sometimes gave rise to bizarre over-eating behaviour, resulting in gross obesity. The hypothalamus is a small but vitally important area of the brain. Reference to any text dealing in neuroanatomy will show that the hypothalamus forms the floor of the posterior part of the forebrain, and, as its name implies, is situated below the thalamus. One might easily guess at the importance of this small area of the brain by observing how many neural tracts enter and leave it, making their way to and from the higher centres of the cerebral cortex as well as the more posterior portions of the brain. The hypothalamus is also directly connected with the pituitary gland by means of the pituitary stalk. All this means that the hypothalamus is uniquely suited to the measurement of metabolic changes and the initiation of regulating activity. It was, then, to the hypothalamus that researchers turned when they wished to look for central nervous system mechanisms in the regulation of not only eating, but other biological motivation such as thirst, sex, and sleep. Indeed, in an influential paper, Stellar (1954) put forward an entire physiological theory of motivation based on the hypothalamus's functional pre-eminence in the general regulation of motivated behaviour.

With regard to eating behaviour, attention first centred on nuclei of cells in the ventromedial area of the hypothalamus. With the advent of stereotaxic techniques it became possible to create lesions in exact placements. Ventromedial lesions were shown reliably to reproduce the anecdotally observed syndrome which we mentioned in the brain-damaged patients earlier. Lesioned rats in this case became hyperphagic — that is to say they over-ate — and rapidly became grossly obese. At first it was thought that a motivational centre had been discovered, a switch, as it were, which controlled hunger. However an important study by Miller, Bailey, and Stevenson (1950) soon dispelled this possibility. While it was true that ventromedially lesioned animals would eat to excess when food was freely available, it was also the case that the same animals were less motivated to obtain food when measures were taken of how much effort-expenditure or aversive stimulation would be tolerated in the process. Results generally continued to suggest that ventromedially lesioned animals do not behave like genuinely hungry animals. They are bad at 'working' for food, and they are also very selective about what they eat: if quinine is added to food to make it more bitter lesioned rats will tolerate much less quinine than will normal rats. In other words hyperphagic rats are particularly taste sensitive. Over all then, it seems that ventromedially lesioned animals, while not motivated to search out food, do have some sort of satiety defect, such that once they have started eating they are unresponsive, in the short term at least, to normal signals of repletion. This conclusion is justified by examining how the animals overeat: in essence they increase meal size rather than meal frequency.

Soon after the discovery of the ventromedial area as a relevant anatomical site, other researchers were finding evidence of self-starvation (aphagia) being linked to lesions in the lateral hypothalamus. As was the case with overeating, it was necessary for researchers now to ask whether refusal to eat in aphagic animals had any motivational properties. It turns out that the lateral hypothalamus has genuine motivational significance. Aphagic animals have a distinct aversion to food (and water — which reminds us that although we are concentrating mainly on eating rather than drinking the two activities are highly related in terms of motivation).

Corroborative evidence linking the lateral hypothalamus to hunger motivation can be seen when we move away from lesion studies and examine electrical stimulation studies. When cells in the lateral hypothalamus are stimulated not only will animals eat food which is given to them, they will learn new responses to obtain food (Coons, Levak, and Miller 1965). They will also pass the other motivational tests which the hyperphagic rats failed: they will tolerate more quinine in their food, for example. Finally, rats which have already fed to satiety will resume eating when cells in the lateral hypothalamus are stimulated.

This impressive array of evidence led to the so-called dual centre theory of hunger motivation being put forward. Basically the lateral hypothalamus is seen as a kind of on-switch for hunger, leading to food-seeking and eating. Ingestion of food leads to metabolic changes (for example, levels of arterial blood sugar and fats) which are signalled back to the ventromedial hypothalamus, which in turn acts as an off-switch to terminate eating.

No sooner had the theory been advanced as a summary of the evidence than it came under attack from critics. The evidence from lesion studies was particularly problematic, since the lateral lesions most effective in producing aphagia were precisely those which may well have damaged adjacent fibre pathways; indeed damage to fibre pathways outside the lateral hypothalamus could also produce aphagia. Such damage, however, also produced a more general dysfunction of orientation to visual and somatosensory stimuli, including food. Thus at least some of the lesion studies could be given a far less hunger-specific interpretation. In the case of stimulation studies it was also found that similar motivational effects on eating behaviour could be obtained from stimulation sites *outside* the lateral hypothalamus in the surrounding limbic system. Balanced against such criticism is the fact that such sites give rise to milder effects (Blundell 1975). However few researchers nowadays would wish to see two distinct regions of the hypothalamus as 'control centres' in the simple way suggested by the dual centre theory. Rather, hypothalamic sites are functionally central to a wider system of regulating circuits involving extra-hypothalamic structures and involving a degree of complexity not envisaged by the simple dual centre theory.

APPETITE AND PREFERENCE

Much recent work has emphasized the importance of using electrical recording techniques (Rolls 1981). Specific populations of neurones have been discovered in the lateral hypothalamus which respond only to the sight of food. Moreover response increases for particularly preferred foods, but ceases if the animal is satiated. Other neurones selectively respond according to the taste rather than the sight of food. Both types of neurone have been shown to be specific with regard to satiation effects. That is to say, satiation with a certain food will gradually lead to a cessation of responding, but this can be reinstated by a new food. What in the end is most important about these cells is that their functioning is predictive of eating behaviour. Neuronal responding is associated with food acceptance, non-responding with food rejection. As Rolls (1981) points out, this gives us the prediction — confirmed in rats and humans — that the total amount consumed is greater when a variety of foods are available. The mechanisms that ensure this must have evolutionary importance, probably ensuring that the individual takes in a wide range of essential nutrients when the opportunity offers. However in any modern society where food is easily available this 'sensory-specific satiety' is probably a factor in fostering obesity.

Another population of lateral hypothalamic neurones respond when food reward is given to an animal. These neurones seem to reflect specifically the rewarding pleasurable aspect of food, since animals will work for direct stimulation of these cells, bypassing the actual receipt of food, as it were. The cells do not respond if the animal is satiated, and self-stimulation rates are also lessened in such circumstances. It is interesting to note the proximity of the lateral hypothalamus to the medial forebrain bundle, which provides the richest source of sites for the self-stimulation studies initiated by Olds and Milner in 1954. These so called 'pleasure centres' clearly are concerned with the reinforcement aspects of a number of motivational systems, though the term 'centres' is a misnomer in this context too, since complex and as yet unmapped circuitry is involved (Redgrave and Dean 1981).

We have just seen that the sight of food excites the lateral hypothalamus and is asssociated with receptiveness to food, especially highly preferred palatable food. Equally associated with the activation of the lateral hypothalamus are reflexive activities in the body itself, notably production of saliva, gastric juices, pancreatic enzymes, and insulin. Lateral hypothalamic activity is directly reflective of this so-called 'cephalic' reflex activity (Powley 1977). But the lateral hypothalamus is also responsive to unpalatable food which prompts another collection of cephalic reflexes, including gagging and vomiting. If we see the ventromedial hypothalamus as involved in inhibiting the intensity of both kinds of cephalic response to food, we begin to see why the ventromedially lesioned hyperphagic animals, mentioned earlier, overate when food was immediately in sight and palatable, but were far more intolerant of unpalatable food.

In essence we are now recognizing the importance of the appetizing facet of food in regulating the amount of food actually consumed. However, appetite can also regulate specific eating. It is known that animals who are deficient in certain vital nutrients will often develop specific preferences for foods rich in the required nutrients. This is thought to be mediated by taste factors. More generally, cephalic responses associated with appetite can be conditioned (for a detailed review and discussion of this area see Booth 1981).

A series of seminal experiments on conditioned taste aversion was carried out by Garcia and his colleagues. Garcia and Koelling (1966) gave rats one of two 'conditioned stimuli' — either a taste cue (saccharin) or an audiovisual cue (light and tone) — followed by one of two aversive consequences — either pain (electric shock) or nausea (irradiation). Among the nauseated rats taste aversion to saccharin was demonstrated, but not fear of light and tone. For the rats exposed to shock, the opposite picture emerged: fear of light and tone but no aversion to saccharin. It seems that taste is particularly easily associated with nausea. Since Garcia and Koelling's early experiment much more work has been done on taste conditioning, much of which serves to emphasize the evolutionary adaptiveness of taste conditioning. Animals generally have a built-in caution with regard to new tastes — a sort of neophobia which we call bait-shyness in the case of troublesome rodents who avoid human-made traps. Only small quantities of 'new' food are eaten. If novel tastes are compared with familiar tastes in an aversive conditioning procedure of the type just outlined it is found that novel tastes lead more easily to the development of conditioned aversion than familiar tastes do. Appetite, then, is a very important factor in guiding food regulation from the point of view of steering animals in the direction of needed foodstuffs and avoiding potentially dangerous ones. A study of its physiology and psychology is an area worthy of increased attention (Booth 1981).

PERSPECTIVES ON OVEREATING

We have already mentioned certain points which might be relevant to the current endemic problem of obesity in societies where a large portion of the population have ready access to food *ad libitum*. Thus diversity of freely available foods may well capitalize on and subvert the purpose of neural mechanisms which would be adaptive in a world of greater scarcity, where the motto might be: eat as much and as diversely as you can while the chance offers itself. Similarly, as soon as we recognize the possibilities of taste conditioning, it is easy to see how appetite (as well as aversions) can be triggered by external situations, sights, smells, etc. In terms of eating motivation, we are a far cry from early theories which stressed only internal cues of deprivation; these are now seen as only part of the picture.

A further perspective on obesity was offered in the 1970s by one of psychology's most innovative researchers, Stanley Schachter. In a widely read article in 1971, Schachter claimed to have discovered some extraordinary facts about obese humans and rats, meaning rats made obese by virtue of ventromedial lesions having given rise to hyperphagia. It will be recalled that such rats, although they overeat, are also less willing to expend effort in getting access to food. Schachter demonstrated similarities in obese people.

In an observational study Schachter looked at the use of chopsticks by obese and normal-weight diners in oriental restaurants; normal-weight diners were five times more likely than the obese to opt for chopsticks.

In an experimental study, Schachter pretended to subjects that the purpose of an experiment was to fill in questionnaires. However, Schachter arranged that subjects had a bag of nuts on their desks either shelled or unshelled. If the nuts were shelled obese subjects ate more than normal subjects. If however the nuts were unshelled the obese subjects hardly touched them.

A subtle addendum to the message of these two studies is that it is not the absolute amount of effort expenditure which seems important, but extra effort relative to an expected norm. Thus orientals who are obese do not switch to western cutlery; nor do we find obese/normal differences in willingness to remove wrappers from chocolates.

Schachter pulled a theory out of such findings and observations, namely that the eating behaviour of obese people (and hyperphagic rats) was largely under the control of external factors (for example, time of day, sight of food, palatability of food) coupled to a relative insensitivity to internal cues of hunger. Schachter's theory about obesity went further however in suggesting that obese people are more generally influenced by external stimuli of all kinds: they are hypothesized to be 'stimulus bound'. In Schachter's own words (1971): 'It may be useful to more generally characterize the obese as stimulus bound and to hypothesize that any stimulus, above a given intensity level, is more likely to evoke an appropriate response from an obese than from a normal subject.'

Attractive as it is, Schachter's generalized theory has proven difficult to support (see Rodin 1981). Some of the problems are definitional. We have seen for example that taste cues and palatability of food are influenced by the state of the organism, and yet such cues were originally conceptualized as external in terms of the theory. Schachter's theory predicts obese/normal differences to depend on intensity of cues, but intensity is hard to define as a dimension along which cues differ. A summary of the evidence suggests that obese and normal-weight subjects differ reliably on palatability effects, but on little else. Although the notion of externally responsive persons has some mileage in it, it is by no means clear that obese people reliably fall into that category. Thus sampling differences may well account for studies which find effects and those which do not.

The notion of external responsiveness, however, prompted Nisbett (1972) to outline another hypothesis with regard to obesity. Nisbett proposed that every individual has an ideal weight or set-point which physiologically the body tries to maintain. Obese people simply are unfortunate in having a higher than normal set-point. There are parallels here again with the hyperphagic rats, which do not go on eating until they explode; rather they go through a dynamic phase in which they overeat until a new obese body-weight is reached, after which they will eat to maintain this new weight within close homeostatic boundaries. Applying the theory to obese people, Nisbett predicts that in trying constantly to bring their weight into culturally approved limits they are paradoxically 'underweight' with respect to their biological set-point, even when they actually appear still to be overweight. Nisbett believed that the stimulus-bound eating patterns of obese persons, in so far as they exist, stem from the continuous exercise of restraint on eating and drew parallels with the known eating habits of starving animals. Finally the theory sees the set-point of an individual as determined by the number of fat cells in the person's body, a factor which is determined largely by genetic endowment and nutritional experience in early infancy.

There are problems with Nisbett's theory, not least the fact that the number of fat cells in the body is not necessarily immutable in adulthood. Additionally Rodin, Slochower, and Fleming (1977) could find no increase in external responsiveness with weight loss in an empirical test of Nisbett's prediction. The concept of the obese person defending a set weight, however, may still be a valid one, and Nisbett has helped to draw attention to the way in which the exercise of dietary restraint itself may help determine eating behaviour. Herman and Polivy (1980) have developed a 'disinhibition hypothesis' which proposes that the self-control of restrained eaters, obese or otherwise, may be temporarily disrupted by disinhibiting situations. Such states may be cognitive in nature, particularly the awareness of having transgressed in one's diet; they may be emotional upsets; or they may be the taking of drugs such as alcohol. The result of disinhibition can be a rebound from restrained eating to going on a binge, and the ultimate in binge eating is seen in cases of bulimia, where the unfortunate individuals will often eat vast quantities of food, deliberately make themselves sick, and start all over again.

Less bizarre overeating can be induced in the laboratory, which gives support to Herman and Polivy's hypothesis. Typically, restrained eaters and unrestrained ones are invited to participate in what is described as a taste test. Half the subjects receive, prior to the test, a calorific drink such as a milk shake. All subjects then sample ice-creams and comment on taste, etc. The real interest of the experimenter is to weigh the subjects' containers before and after the taste session to assess the exact quantity of ice cream consumed during the tasting. Results tend to confirm that with a milk shake pre-load restrained eaters eat more than without the pre-load, whereas unrestrained eaters show the opposite pattern which we might consider more to be expected, namely eating less in the tasting session if already pre-loaded with a milk shake.

Unfortunately at present the literature does not suggest that the disinhibition hypothesis much illuminates problems of obesity (Ruderman 1986). While obese subjects do show higher restraint scores than normals they do not behave like the non-obese restrained eaters described above, so in their specific case disinhibition does not seem to be responsible for overeating. In fact it is now generally believed that no one simple theory is going to account for a neat single homogeneous group of people labelled obese. The restraint hypothesis has however more relevance to anorexia and bulimia, especially since bulimia is part of the presenting picture in about half of all cases of anorexia. Anorexics define themselves through their extreme restraint and so the disinhibition hypothesis would obviously predict that episodes of overeating in the guise of bulimia would indeed occur.

CONCLUSION

This selective review of motivational factors in eating behaviour has had as its main intention the discussion of what is commonly considered a biological motive par excellence — the motive to eat. It is clear that even in the case of putative biological imperatives, psychological and physiological discovery must go hand in hand.

17

3

Sleeping

An activity which accounts for about a third of all our lives has some rights to be considered a biological imperative. And yet the full-square motivational question 'Why do we sleep?' is not one that can be easily answered, despite the fact that much knowledge has accrued about the psychology and physiology of sleep.

SLEEP AND THE EEG

The scientific study of sleep took a large leap forward when the technology of electroencephalography (EEG) was developed. The EEG is a record of the electrical activity of the brain taken from electrodes positioned on the surface of the skull. Brain waves, as they are known, can be graphically portrayed in their differing forms. The normal alert and awake brain typically produces a wave of high frequency and low amplitude, irregular in form. As a person relaxes the wave becomes lower in frequency and the pattern is termed 'alpha activity'. Light sleep sees a further decrease in frequency but with occasional interruptions in the form of higher frequency bursts known as spindles. This move towards lower frequency and higher amplitude continues through what researchers quantify as three stages to the deepest stage 4 sleep, where the spindles have virtually vanished and the EEG shows a 'delta' pattern': very slow high amplitude waves, quite different from the waking pattern.

There is one paradoxical picture however that emerges as the EEG of a sleeping subject is monitored. Periodically the EEG changes completely to a pattern that resembles the waking one, and at the same time rapid eye movements occur (REM). During such periods the subject is however most deeply asleep, as measured by the criterion of sensitivity to external stimuli and ease of waking. Furthermore this so-called REM sleep is characterized by far more reports of dreaming than are produced when sleepers are woken from periods of non-REM sleep.

HOW WE SLEEP

With the EEG, then, we have an objective means of determining when people are sleeping and what stage of sleep they are in. This is an important fact, since people's own reports of when they have been sleeping are notoriously unreliable; the insomniac who claims not to have slept a wink is almost always mistaken.

EEG researchers have been able to learn a great deal about 'how' we sleep. During an average night's sleep, the typical experimental subject, with EEG attached, will fairly quickly go through to the deepest stage 4 of non-REM sleep, that is within about half an hour, and will then start climbing back through stage 3 and stage 2. This cycle then continues, except that as the night progresses the amount of time spent in stage 4 sleep significantly falls off, so that by the second half of the night virtually no time is given over to this stage. Contrarily, paradoxical or REM sleep is present only for short periods in the early part of the night but makes longer and longer appearances as time goes on and follows on from periods of stage 2 sleep.

If we look at patterns of sleep on a longer term basis we also see differences in the amount of time allocated to REM and non-REM sleep. Thus REM sleep forms a much larger percentage of total sleep in the very young and gradually falls off through childhood and adolescence to reach a plateau of about 25 per cent in adulthood. Stage 4 sleep stabilizes at about 15 per cent, while stage 2 sleep occupies by far the largest period, averaging about half of all sleep. These of course are averages and individual variability exists especially among the elderly, both with respect to total sleeping time and type of sleep.

BRAIN MECHANISMS CONTROLLING SLEEP

Although the question of why we need to sleep is not so obviously answerable as the question of why we need to eat, it is still the case that physiological psychologists have located areas of the brain which seem to have a controlling function in sleeping behaviour, just as they have discovered areas associated with eating.

19

Much work in the 1950s increased our knowledge of the role of the Reticular Activating System (RAS) in the determination of wakefulness and sleep (Moruzzi 1964). The RAS is a dense network of neurons lying in the subcortical structures of the brain, extending from the medulla of the lower brain-stem to the thalamus. High frequency electrical stimulation of the RAS induces both EEG and behavioural arousal in a sleeping animal. If on the other hand the brain-stem higher up is sectioned then the result is a behaviourally comatose animal. This 'waking centre' is known after its discoverers as 'the ascending reticular activating system of Moruzzi and Magoun'. However, it would be wrong to conclude that sleep is the mere absence of wakefulness. We have seen already that the brain in REM sleep is far from inactive, although it is then at its most impervious to the intrusion of external stimuli. In non-REM sleep it is known that the brain continues to monitor much that goes on in the external world of sound. Oswald (1966) reported that subjects often wake up in response to 'relevant' auditory inputs. For example a mother may wake to the merest sound of a troubled infant but sleep right through the overhead, much noisier flight of a jumbo jet; all of us are more than likely to respond to our own names. Thus sleep is not in any of its forms to be identified as an absence of consciousness; rather it is an altered state of consciousness.

More recently therefore, investigators have concentrated on exploring brain structures which may be specifically and actively involved in inducing and maintaining sleep. One of the pioneers in such work has been the French scientist Michel Jouvet. The search for areas actively associated with sleep has pointed to the importance of two particular areas: the raphe nuclei which lie along the midline of the brain-stem, and, once again in the brain-stem, at the level of the pons, an area called the locus coerulus.

Destruction of the raphe nuclei leads to a virtually permanently awake organism, whilst different degrees of damage tend to be correlated with different degrees of impaired sleep functioning. The locus coerulus was initially highlighted by Jouvet (1967) as a controlling centre specifically for REM sleep, since destruction in this area seems selectively to impair REM sleep. Further research of a biochemical kind suggests that these two sleep areas are further differentiated in terms of the chemical transmitter substances used by their neurons: the raphe nuclei contain serotonin, while the locus coerulus is rich in noradrenalin.

Although such work on central mechanisms involved in the control of sleep continues to develop, it will no doubt have become clear that there is a vacuum which makes our discussion very different so far from our discussion of eating behaviour. In that discussion we assumed that mechanisms were sensitive to a whole variety of signals, which in turn were bedded in physiological need. We can no longer put off the fundamental question: does sleep fulfil some basic survival need, and if so what?

A NEED FOR SLEEP

A plausible reason for the existence of sleep might be to rest the body. In layman's terms, one rests in order to alleviate or avoid fatigue. However as far as physical relaxation is concerned there are far better ways of relaxing muscles than actually going to sleep. Moreover a videotaped record of a person's sleeping would reveal much tossing and turning, and plenty of muscle activity. What then about relaxing the brain? Once again the use of the word 'relaxation' is suspect: we have seen already that plenty of neuronal activity goes on throughout a period of sleep but is of a different pattern, except for REM sleep, from the waking one. Thus sleep is not characterized by any major decrease in neural activity, just a change in it.

Some researchers have suggested an evolutionary reason for sleep to have developed so readily in the animal kingdom — it is for example universal among mammals. The argument suggests that survival would have been enhanced for those animals which succumb to a period of inactivity, usually coinciding with darkness, where energy resources are conserved and encounters with predators and other external dangers are minimized at a time when sensory acuity is not at its best.

This is a plausible speculation, but once again we are left mystified about the aspects of sleep which go beyond mere inactivity. Could the physical organism actually be 'doing' something vital to its survival during sleep? There has been a tradition of theories suggesting that some toxin or other accumulates through the waking hours and has to be broken down and removed during sleep. However no such toxin has been discovered.

Let us then pursue a psychological argument for a moment, and let us consider an individual as an information processor. Any information processor has to have facilities for receiving input, coding it, storing it, and retrieving it. Moreover one bit of input relates to another: memory in the waking brain is highly organized. However the individual is not simply reducible to an information processor, but is also a user of information in the service of pursuing pleasures

21

and avoiding pains. When this busy user finally falls asleep could it be that, just like the computer centre at work, the brain must at times take itself 'off-line' and refuse to handle any more jobs until it has organized new inputs into its store? Psychologists have long spoken of material being consolidated into a long-term and virtually permanent memory. Could sleep be a vital aid in the consolidation process?

The psychological theory has a physiological substrate. Following Hebb's (1966) influential ideas of short-term temporary storage being electrical (firing circuits of neurons) but long-term storage being chemical, we can see the consolidation process as chemical work being done. One major view is that protein synthesis is intimately involved in long-term memory (Flood *et al*. 1981). Does sleep promote such synthesis? One way to investigate this question and other more general questions concerning our need to sleep, is to deprive volunteer subjects of this vital commodity.

SLEEP DEPRIVATION STUDIES

Psychology can often learn a great deal from anecdotal evidence, so we begin with the tale of Frank Mulville, who, taking his yacht back from Iceland to his home port in Essex, came close to shipwreck at the very last moment, within a few miles of his mooring and in waters known like the back of his hand. The culprit: sleep deprivation.

It is the brain that is slowed and dulled by fatigue, not the body. However tired, the body will work until it drops but the signals it receives from the brain become slow, confused, misleading. A fatigued brain will pretend it isn't tired, that it has infinite resources of stamina to draw on. A fatigued brain is easily disorientated; it halluncinates, it destroys our sense of balance, it no longer co-ordinates with the body. . .

Then I saw something strange to leeward. It was a sort of hump, shaped like half a sausage cut longways. I watched it fascinated — perhaps it was a cloud, or some sort of ship; it couldn't be the land of course, there's nothing like that on Mersea. I must have watched it for at least one minute — times loses all urgency and meaning when you're exhausted. Slowly, like a stone sinking through mud, it occurred to me that I ought to put Iskra about. 'Yes,' I thought to myself, 'yes — I think I'll put her about.' I nodded to myself, still watching the hump, mesmerized. Then I reached down to the tiller, threw off the chain for the self-steering, and put the helm down. Iskra struck the shingle at that precise moment . . . . The half sausage was the high shingle bank on the end of Colne point.

(Mulville 1986)

Many other 'case histories' could be quoted to testify to the havoc wreaked by prolonged sleep deprivation on persons required to handle complex inputs of information. Prosaic as it may be to turn now to the laboratory, it is in the laboratory that we can study more exactly some of the deficits induced by measured amounts of sleep deprivation.

A classic experiment was performed by Jenkins and Dallenbach (1924). They required two subjects to learn lists of nonsense syllables and then to recall them eight hours later. Subjects showed superior recall if the lists had been learned in the evening rather than the morning, that is, when sleep had intervened between learning and recall. It is possible therefore that sleep aids the consolidation of new material, whereas a waking period produces interference effects which militate against consolidation.

Unfortunately Jenkins and Dallenbach's simple experiment has other interpretations. Sleep periods took place normally and at night. It is thus possible that other factors, coinciding with night-time, were responsible for their results. For example, the circulating hormones, cortisol, adrenalin, and noradrenalin, are at their lowest ebb during the night and it is known that all of these have an inhibitory effect on the synthesis of new protein, which we have seen has been linked to long-term memory consolidation. To show that sleep has a direct and positive effect on learning and memory processes, it is necessary to rule out the effects of other 'circadian' variations, as they are called.

A recent series of experiments by Idzikowski (1984) provides more compelling evidence that sleep is directly involved in promoting memory consolidation. In these experiments subjects were genuinely deprived of sleep, as opposed simply to being studied after sleep-free periods.

The crucial comparison in Idzikowski's experiment was between two groups of subjects. One group learned a list of nonsense syllables one morning and were tested for recall the following morning, but were deprived of sleep during the night. The other group was identically treated except that they were allowed their normal sleep in between sessions. The presence of sleep led to 17 per cent better retention, which was statistically highly significant. Note that over a twenty-four-hour period no circadian variation factors existed between the groups, thus leaving us to conclude that the sleep factor

23

was responsible for the difference found. Idzikowski also ran some further comparison groups, in which time of retrieval varied both for sleep-deprived and non-deprived groups, thus enabling the researcher to see whether, notwithstanding the demonstrated effects of sleep, there might also be effects due to interference and circadian variation at the time of retrieval. No such effects were found.

However, the undeniable and crucial difference between the two key groups could be argued to be due to some non-specific factors resulting from sleep deprivation, but operating on the efficiency with which items are retrieved and not on the assumed consolidating processes. This Idzikowski examined in a further experiment, in which all subjects learned a list of nonsense syllables in the evening of day 1 and recalled them on the morning of day 3 (a thirty-three-hour interval). Both groups slept between day 1 and day 2, that is, when consolidation processes were hypothesized to be active, but one group was deprived of sleep during the night between day 2 and day 3. If sleep deprivation were indeed affecting retrieval efficiency then this group should have fared worse on the morning of day 3. If, however, sleep only affects consolidation processes soon after input of material then no difference should be observed between the groups, despite the later sleep deprivation. No difference was observed, thus giving support to the consolidation theory.

In these experiments we are seeing that even mild sleep deprivation can be demonstrably linked to measureable cognitive impairment. This contradicts some of the claims of earlier sleep deprivation researchers that sleep deprivation had no such effects. The truth would appear to be that much depends on what behaviour is looked at. Highly skilled or demanding tasks are more easily affected than simpler or well practised ones. There is also a high degree of variability in the effects induced by sleep deprivation. It seems hardly necessary to point out that some individuals seem to need much more or less than others. We should also add that the effects of deprivation are very quickly reversed. Case histories of long sleep deprivation feats, aimed at the record books, show that one or two good nights' sleep make up immediately for many more lost nights.

REM-SPECIFIC DEPRIVATION

Since it is invariably the case that REM sleep is entered after a preceding period of non-REM sleep, it is quite possible to deprive an individual of REM sleep without unduly disturbing total sleep. This is done by waking the individual at the moment REM begins, knowing that another cycle of non-REM sleep will intervene before the next REM episode. Such subjects can be compared with controls who are similarly disrupted but during periods of non-REM sleep. Such techniques have been used to find out whether there is any evidence of a specific need for REM sleep.

If evidence for a need is given by subjects trying selectively to make up for REM deprivation, there certainly seems to be such a need. Dement (1960) first demonstrated this by showing that REM deprived subjects over a five night period needed waking increasingly often to prevent their going into REM sleep. On the final two nights of the experiment all subjects were allowed to sleep normally. The REM deprived subjects, but not the controls, spent about 60 per cent more time than usual in REM sleep. This so-called REM rebound effect has been confirmed in later experiments.

The early results from Dement's laboratory also suggested that REM deprived groups found the procedure far more discomforting than non-REM deprived. They were more irritable and anxious and there were even some reports of bizarre and hallucinatory experiences following REM deprivation. However the argument for emotional impairment is much less clear-cut than for selective rebound. And yet the anecdotal evidence such as that with which we began, where fatigue and environmental demands are at levels not reached in any ethically approved laboratory, does point to sensory and even hallucinatory experiences which it is difficult to avoid linking with deprivation of 'dream' sleep. Since however such natural subjects are obviously not selectively deprived it must remain a supposition that REM deprivation is responsible for dream-like phenomena.

As if, however, to show how complex affairs can be, there is literature (see Vogel 1975) which suggests that in some cases deprivation of REM sleep can be associated with improvement in depressive symptoms. When we consider such factors as different base levels, degree of deprivation, context, and no doubt a host of individual difference variables, it is perhaps not unsurprising that REM deprivation has been linked to both positive and negative emotional effects.

It is easier perhaps to point the finger at REM deprivation with regard to the memory deficits which we have already mentioned. Recall of material learned on one day is usually found to be poorer following REM deprivation (Tilley and Empson 1978; Tilley 1981). Taken with Idzikowski's results the implication is that REM sleep may be particularly involved in memory consolidation.

DREAMING

Finally we come to a discussion of what through the ages has been a source of mystery to every generation, a mystery not yet to be dispelled by this or any other text. The corollary of our last section, if we take REM sleep to be 'dream' sleep, is that dreaming is an experiential by-product of our attempts to consolidate our daily experiences. Perhaps. We must however be wary of too readily seeing a parallel between the physical reality of REM and the experiential world of dreams. While it is true that vivid dream reports are linked to persons' waking from REM periods, it is by no means the case that dream reports are absent when waking from non-REM periods. The reports are less frequent and the dream material can usually be described as less interesting, but it does exist.

We cannot leave the topic of dreaming, however, without some mention of Sigmund Freud's classic, *The Interpretation of Dreams* (1900). Freud, more than most great thinkers, was forever interested in finding meaning in, not to say imposing it on, experience. Nowhere is this seen more clearly than in his theory of dreaming. No doubt before Joseph obliged the Pharaoh with his prophecy of seven years of plenty and seven of famine, men and women were eager to find meaning in their dreams. For recent generations Freudian theory has seemed a means of achieving this.

The purpose of dreams for Freud was to express wishes which could not be fully recognized in conscious waking life. In accordance with the rest of his theory, such wishes sprang from libidinal impulses. However, even in dreams the sexual content had to be disguised through symbolism and distortions of one kind or another, censored as it were from being so obvious as to wake and alert the conscious mind. Thus Freud distinguished the manifest content of the dream (which he noted often referred to events of the previous day) from the latent content of the dream, which harked back to unconscious wishes bedded in libidinal conflicts.

Freud no doubt would not be surprised to learn that in the case of males, be they infants or adults, REM sleep is invariably accompanied by genital erection. Unfortunately however the dreams reported on waking the subject often show a total absence of any sexual content. The Freudian response might be to invoke symbolism and disguise, but that of course is a road which leads to the theory being unfalsifiable — if there always could be disguised sexual content then we have no means of saying what would constitute a non-sexual dream. The trouble with Freud's theory is that it is dogmatic: all dreams are wish fulfilments, and all dreams have a correct interpretation which leads the psychoanalyst down the so-called 'royal road' to the unconscious. And yet modern cognitive psychologists know enough about the diversity and complexity of long-term memory organization to be less dogmatic about what is happening in REM sleep. Our memories do interlock across networks of shared meanings and associations; such meanings and associations can be unconscious and they can be emotional. In the laboratory, fully awake subjects can react physiologically to a threat-associated word which they have not consciously registered; tastes and smells, as Marcel Proust so well describes, can evoke keen emotional response through associations half a lifetime dead. If REM sleep has something to do with memory consolidation then it is not implausible to suggest that dream fragments might be telling us something about how a living sentient — and even libidinal — being is trying to order his or her latest round of meaningful experiences.

CONCLUSIONS

Sleeping and dreaming are activities which remain deeply mysterious. We have reviewed evidence which tells us a great deal about the patterning of these activities. We even have some theoretical notion of their possible role in memory consolidation processes. But comprehensive theories, particularly of dreaming, elude us. Freud's pioneering attempt at a grand theory fails. Current psychological theories have the look of highly speculative attempts to put together a jigsaw puzzle with half the pieces still missing and no real idea of what constitutes the border of the picture.

4

Sex

The motive which Sigmund Freud saw as causing neurosis and shaping civilization in a supposed extravaganza of unconscious activity is not something to be dismissed lightly, even if few academic psychologists would now come anywhere near describing themselves as Freudians. Even if we avoid discussing the meaning of 'unconscious sexual motivation' and concern ourselves solely with consciously experienced sexual phenomena it nevertheless remains difficult to say exactly how pervasive a motive that bald word 'sex' signifies.

In this chapter we are concerned primarily with human motivation, so why do we not begin with the obviously scientific approach of measuring how much time the average human being spends in sexual activity during the course of the average day? After all, this essentially is the approach that Premack and others have taken in the area of reinforcement theory to gauge the relative importance and value of such rodent activities as eating and wheel-turning. A difficulty is immediately apparent: what are we going to take as constituting sexual activity? Counting acts of coitus is going to give us an extremely conservative estimate of sexual activity. If we include any activity which results in orgasm we are still being restrictive. Even a caricature version of a behaviourist would have to admit that time spent in sexual fantasy should be admitted, as well as time spent on any number of daily provided sources of titillation. For students of human sexual motivation the interesting questions centre on individual variation in the parameters of sexual activity: the fact is that humans show large individual differences in the extent to which they pursue sexual goals as well as the ways in which they seek them.

Although we are primarily concerned with human motivation, sex is clearly seen, at least in the lay mind, as a biological motive *par excellence* — 'that sly biological urge', as Noël Coward once termed it. Certainly overt sexual activity — we cannot speak for fantasy — is something we clearly share with all sexually reproducing organisms, and in that sense the motive or urge has biological roots. However what most authorities agree makes human sexual motivation so different from that found in the rest of the animal kingdom is that it has become largely divorced from the function of reproduction (see, for example, Michelmore 1964, and Barash 1981). There is an analogy here with our review of hunger motivation: in a context of abundant supply, much of the motivation to eat is largely prompted by the stimulation of the appetite by environmental cues. Both sexual activity and eating are highly pleasurable activities which are all too easily indulged if the environment provides the right opportunities. Individual differences in indulgence propensities have much to do with competing motives (to obey a moral code, to keep to a diet, etc.). The idea that in addition individuals vary in the strength of a sex 'drive' is a more difficult matter to assess. Sexual activity does not indicate drive strength, nor even would some curious measure of resistance to sexual temptation, which more likely will reflect the strength of competing societally induced motives. How much is the totally abstinent monk helped by a putative low sex drive and how much by a strong commitment to his vows? He cannot tell us, since he has no way of assessing the strength of his sex drive. If he were totally abstinent and counted the frequency of involuntary nocturnal emissions and knew the population statistics in this regard he might be able to offer some sort of answer, but even that, for reasons I leave the reader to work out, would be a seriously flawed index of something which is beginning to seem metaphysical.

Can physiology more exactly answer the question in terms of sex hormones? In most animals of course there is an intimate link between sexual activity and hormones which reflects the connection between sex and reproduction referred to earlier. Most female mammals, in particular, have cyclical periods of receptivity, hormonally induced, which not surprisingly coincide with periods when conception is most probable. Males do not show such cyclical variation in hormonally induced behaviour but do respond to specific stimuli offered by the receptive females.

The direct effects of hormones on sexual interest and arousal in the case of human beings are far less evident and, most important, are far from simple to interpret. It is certainly the case that men and women are largely liberated from hormonal control of sexual arousal: in neurophysiological terms the neocortex dominates. There is some evidence which might link androgens (male sex hormones) to enhanced

29

sexual desire in both sexes, and certainly female hormones have been used to dampen the sexual drive of male sexual offenders. It may be noted at this point that sex hormones are not uniquely produced by the sex glands specific to either males (testes) or females (ovaries): small quantities of androgens, for example, are produced in females as well as in males via the adrenal cortex. Thus it is quite possible, in the case of human beings at least, that androgens may play some small role in determining levels of sexual interest or libido. There is of course always the perennial problem in trying to marry psychological concepts such as sexual interest to physiological functioning that correlation is always easier to show than causation. The substantive truth is that sexual desire in the normally function- ing human being is largely a result of higher cortical activity and not the expression of some primitive hormonally driven mechanism. Even castrated adult males (who have therefore lost their major source of testosterone, the most potent androgen) are reported in some cases to maintain near normal sexual interest at least for a time. If, by implication, the cortex can in the short term compensate for such gross loss of hormonal functioning, it seems reasonable to suppose that it, rather than small hormone level differences, regulates sexual interest in the intact person. It follows that psychological therapy rather than hormone therapy is likely to be the usual recommendation for those complaining of a loss of libido. It also explains why pedlars of supposed aphrodisiacs are not noted for providing guarantees.

MEN, WOMEN AND SEX

It has been traditional wisdom that, with regard to matters of sexual motivation, men and women are very different. Even Kinsey and his colleagues decided to produce *two* beacons of enlightenment, *Sexual Behavior in the Human Male* (1948) appearing a good few years before the second volume (1953) dealing with the human female. With regard to frequency of sexual activity and particularly with regard to orgasm and masturbation, Kinsey and his colleagues reported substantially less activity in females. Without casting doubt on the accuracy of Kinsey's findings, we need to make two important points. First, sexual behaviour is so powerfully under the influence of cultural and societal norms that it would be quite wrong to assume any really immu- table or significant differences in sexual motivation or interest on the basis of such 'time-capsuled' findings. Second, there is reason to believe, based on more recent surveys, that sex differences in frequency of sexual activity have radically diminished.

Are there any other important differences in the sexual motivation of males and females? Two questions have been addressed by researchers, both of which are prompted by traditional folklore, and both of which relate to what is best expressed by the idiomatic term 'turn-on'. The first question is: Are males naturally more responsive when variety in terms of sexual partners is on offer? The second is: Do men and women respond differently to erotic material? We address each question in turn.

The argument that, for males, variety is the spice of sex has been called the 'Coolidge' effect, if only because it allows authors to relate an amusing anecdote about the notoriously taciturn American president. On a tour of a farm, his wife was told that just one rooster served all the sexual needs of the hen-house. 'Tell that to my husband', she said. On being so informed, the president asked whether the rooster changed partner each time and was told that this was so. 'Tell that to Mrs Coolidge' was his rejoinder.

Indeed, it has been amply demonstrated in the case of many infra-human species that males are highly motivated to run down mazes, and show few satiation effects, so long as the incentive of a new copulatory partner is provided each time. While female animals will also respond to sexual opportunity as a reinforcer, they do not show this pronounced effect of change of partner in rekindling sexual motivation. Of course we must be wary of undue generalization across species, but it must be pointed out that monogamy is a rare condition in mammals and even rarer in those mammals closest to us in evolutionary terms, the primates. As far as anthropology is concerned, monogamy seems to have been an exceedingly recent invention of culturally advanced societies, when measured against the over-all time our species has been on this planet. The speculations of sociobiologists (for example, Dawkins 1976) are also probably less speculative on this issue than on some others: it does seem that there would have to be good overriding reasons — and they in turn can be speculated on — why males should not obey a programme which urges them to scatter their easily dispensed seed as widely as possible, thus encouraging some success on some fertile ground somewhere. The female has a far more careful investment to make, in which mistakes are costly. It pays her to be choosy about a sexual partner. Such cost-benefit analyses do of course seem crude — all the more so when put so baldly — but their logic can support a theoretical stance even if proof is in the nature of things impossible.

Other supportive strands for those who wish to argue the case for

31

a natural streak of promiscuity in the male of our species can be mentioned. It has been commonly observed that sexual fidelity is rarer and promiscuity greater (at least until the current AIDS crisis) among male gays than among lesbians. Within the straight community and also in the pre-AIDS days of the 1960s it is notable that it was husbands rather than wives who initiated membership of 'swinging' groups where sexual boredom could be relieved by mate-swapping (Baron *et al.* 1974). Needless to say such observations are capable of different interpretations, and if we are going to propose with William James that 'higamus, hogamus, Woman is monogamous; hogamus, higamus, Man is polygamous' then it will be on the balance and consistency of different lines of evidence, and certainly not on the basis of any single matter of fact.

Whether females and males respond differently to erotica is an equally difficult question to answer with any degree of exactitude. The Kinsey reports suggested that traditional wisdom was not far off the mark in believing that women are not so aroused by hard core pornography, and respond better to erotic material in a loving and/or romantic setting. Since the 1950s, however, experimental research has fairly conclusively shown otherwise. There are few differences between the sexes either in self-reported arousal or physiological measures when exposed to identical erotic material (Schmidt and Schafer 1973; Sigusch *et al.* 1970). Moreover it seems to be the case that in both sexes the arousal from watching an erotic film is greater if subjects are explicitly told that the couple in the film are not deeply in love but simply behaving out of sexual desire (Byrne and DeNinno 1974).

Conclusive as the experimental research is with regard to the direction of findings, we must nevertheless remain cautious in our interpretation, since subjects taking part in such experiments may not be typical of the population generally. If this is a normal caveat to be issued in relation to all psychology experiments, it is a particularly forceful one in regard to recruiting for experiments involving exposure to erotic material. Given that we would anyway expect individual differences in response to erotica, as a result of upbringing factors, the real message of the laboratory studies has little to do with generalization and everything to do with the demonstration that some women at least do respond quite as clearly as men to purely erotic stimulation, and do not require romance or love to generate sexual interest. Such findings suggest that any sex differences that may in fact exist outside the laboratory reflect the operation of cultural stereotypes and expectations. The number of women in pornography shops may be infinitesimal compared with men and women's magazines may not as a rule display male nudes. It would, however, be a reckless person who inferred from this that women are less responsive to explicit erotica. Every other explanation for such behavioural differences is likely to be nearer the truth.

One final point, however, may be made on this matter. It seems that erotic material only induces sexual arousal in so far as it engages the imagination of the viewer, listener, or reader. While explicit erotic material can arouse males and females equally, this is not of course to say that differences may not exist in the fantasies that are woven around the material. Indeed, in some very obvious ways, it would be strange if there were not differences between males and females in this regard.

SEXUAL VARIATION

Since sexual arousal in humans so massively involves the most developed neocortical areas of the brain, it is not surprising that conditioning and learning generally play a great role in determining what sorts of activities individuals find sexually gratifying. One could therefore produce an almost endless list of the bizarre activities other than coitus, and 'objects' other than a person, which have been reportedly used for sexual gratification. To some generations all such activities would doubtless be seen as 'perversions'. To other generations the parallel we drew between sex and eating would seem apt: certain activities would be seen rather like herbs and spices, or, like chocolates, an occasional indulgence. The ancient and tolerant aphorism *de gustibus non disputandum*', roughly translated as 'there's no arguing about taste', reinforces the parallel with the world of food.

Common fetishes involving fabrics or items of clothing provide good examples of the way that sexual arousal can become conditioned to inherently non-sexual stimuli. They also provide a useful illustration of the uselessness of a medical model which labels such fetishes as forms of pathology. To illustrate the point, let us imagine two persons, both of whom for some reason are immensely turned on by shiny plastic raincoats. In the first case the man (most recorded fetishists are male) has a wife who is reasonably accommodating about such matters. Sometimes, but not necessarily always, they make love when she is attired in unusual garb, and occasionally he masturbates while perusing something from his small library of specialized pornography. Otherwise he is as dull as the proverbial man on the

Clapham omnibus. Is he odd? Perhaps. Is he ill? Clearly not.

Now let us imagine the second man. Unmarried and lonely, he has limited sexual experience, paying prostitutes to indulge what he sees as the unfortunate 'kink' compulsively controlling him. Is he ill? Once again, the answer is no, if by 'ill' we mean something like 'suffering from a fetish'. What this person does have is problems in coming to terms with certain odd sexual desires, but the desires themselves do not constitute an illness. An illuminating though not perfect parallel might be the person who is obese because of a weakness for cream cakes. It is certainly true that the person has a problem, but the problem is not 'liking cream cakes', rather it is 'eating too many of them'. There might of course be further problems if the person felt terrible guilt about liking cream cakes.

There is no better road to greater tolerance about sexual variation within a culture than a proper appreciation of sexual variations between cultures. There are societies where a certain degree of breast fetishism is counted as normal and there are societies where it would not be understood. This is not the appropriate book to give lists of sexual practices as they vary in different cultures (the interested reader may wish to refer to classic works, such as that by Ford and Beach 1951). However the existence of cross-cultural sexual variation is something that should be well noted. We now, however, shall discuss one aspect of sexual variation which is so prevalent and universal that it demands separate consideration: it concerns variation from the norm in the sex of persons to whom one is attracted or, more generally, to whom one is sexually orientated.

SEXUAL ORIENTATION

Kinsey envisaged sexual orientation as a continuum with exclusive heterosexuality at one end and exclusive homosexuality at the other end. In the middle lies bisexuality. How then does this square with the more current tendency for people to think in terms of categories, where bisexuality is rather lost in a seemingly universal agreement to divide the world into 'gay' and 'straight'?

The apparent contradiction between continuum and typology is resolved when we take more than simple sexual preference into account. So strong is the prejudice against gays — in some cases so pathological as to be termed 'homophobia' (Weinberg 1975) — that it is not surprising that the majority of persons who have at least some heterosexual feelings tend to define themselves as 'straight', and avoid any expression, at least openly, of homosexual feelings. Indeed the pressure in society to conform to the heterosexual norm is so great that many persons who, on Kinsey's scale, would be exclusively homosexual nevertheless get married and try to pass for 'straight', confining their homosexual activity to secretive encounters. Even they, however, might privately label themselves 'gay', suggesting that this is a typology which principally involves people recognizing that they feel little attraction to the opposite sex and great attraction to the same sex. The word 'gay', however, clearly is used by openly 'come-out' gays themselves to indicate not just their sexual orientation, but their positive acceptance of who and what they are.

What percentage of the population is predominantly homosexual? In the case of males, the figure is probably of the order of 5 per cent and in the case of females more like 2 per cent. These are the sorts of figures that reliably crop up in the surveys, including Kinsey's own massive research. However all figures in this area of research will remain difficult to be sure about so long as sampling is plagued by societal prejudice. Certainly homosexual *behaviour* is much more common than is implied by these estimates of numbers of persons identifying themselves as homosexual. Kinsey's figures are still prob- ably the most trustworthy: one in eight males have had more homosexual than heterosexual experience for at least three years between the ages of 16 and 55, while two males out of every five have during the same time had at least some homosexual experience to the point of orgasm. Such homosexual behaviour is also, to use Kinsey's phrase, 'more than incidental'. Clearly there seems to be a lot more homosexual behaviour about than persons willing to call themselves homosexual, certainly among males. Homosexuality is something which seems to be part of all human societies, and always has been, although its manner and degree of expression have varied. Among other species, in particular primates, homosexual behaviour also occurs regularly, although the notion of homosexual identity is meaningless in such a context.

What factors determine a person's predominant sexual orientation? Until recently this question was addressed in a lop-sided way, in terms of the causes of homosexuality. Such an approach ignores the wider and more proper question about how heterosexuality as well as homosexuality is established.

By tortuous reasoning, involving Oedipal conflict and fixation, Freudians maintain that homosexual males have overattentive mothers and weak or absent fathers. This is based as far as one can tell on the totally questionable assumption that the handful of homosexual men that have sought treatment from psychoanalysts are in any way representative of the 'gay' community as a whole. What homophobic individuals will undoubtedly like about psychoanalytic theory is that it implies that homosexuality is a form of immaturity which hetero-sexuals grow out of. However, it would surely be difficult for any fair-minded judge, faced with two random samples of historically famed homosexuals and heterosexuals, to find any evidence of greater maturity in the latter, unless in true circular fashion homosexuality itself was taken *ipso facto* as a sign of psychic damage and immaturity.

Conditioning theory suggests that sexual orientation is determined quite simply by the pattern of pleasurable and painful encounters that a person is exposed to. We are asked to envisage that a person who has some pleasurable homosexual experiences and some anxiety-provoking heterosexual ones, gradually builds on the former and comes to avoid the latter.

The theory falters on certain key points. Why is homosexuality so pervasive despite the enormous incentives to persevere in becoming heterosexual? One would surely expect that if everyone had some potential for heterosexuality, they would go to great lengths to develop that potential. Indeed in the past some homosexuals have gone to great lengths to seek 'treatment' for their condition. The 'success rates' of all methods, including those claiming to be based on conditioning principles, have been low; more to the point, the criteria of success have been inadequate. Finally, what 'success' is achieved seems to depend critically on whether or not any pleasurable heterosexual experiences have occurred prior to treatment (Ellis and Ames 1987), which could be taken to mean that successful 'treatment' is only possible when one gets the 'diagnosis' wrong in the first place. Finally, if alteration of orientation is possible one way round it should be equally possible the other way round. Although there is evidence that, in certain types of all-male establishments such as prisons and boarding schools, much homosexual behaviour takes place, there is no evidence to suggest that previously heterosexual prisoners who participate do not return to heterosexual preference when they are released, nor in the case of adolescent boarders is homosexual behaviour an infallible guide to later orientation; often it simply reflects sexual experimentation and probably extraversion. It does not seem therefore that homosexual experience shapes homosexual orientation in any simple fashion.

If sexual orientation, especially when exclusive preference exists, is so difficult to alter, might this not suggest the importance of biological bases of some kind? There is certainly some evidence that genetic factors might be involved in determining sexual orientation. Pillard *et al.* (1982) found that nearly a quarter of all brothers of male homosexuals were also homosexual. This figure is about five times what we would expect from our knowledge of average population incidence. The likely influence of genetic factors is indirect, and most biologically based theories about the development of sexual orientation place importance on the role of hormones on the developing nervous system during gestation. Genetic factors may influence this development. What evidence is there for a neurohormonal theory of sexual orientation?

There are certainly no obvious hormonal differences between homosexual and heterosexual individuals in levels of sex hormones, such as testosterone, produced after puberty. It is during gestation that hormonal factors may be important. Certainly in animal studies, including those involving primates, homosexual behaviour can be induced as the norm in the adult, if while still a foetus it is exposed to large amounts of androgens or estrogens, depending on its genetic sex. Equally such effects can be duplicated by blocking or enhancing the effects of the naturally occurring hormones.

The argument goes that genetic sex only provides a blueprint for development. Depending on hormone levels at critical stages, males and females develop differently along quite separate dimensions: they come to differ in regard to external genitalia and other morphological features such as muscle mass, but also in regard to behaviour-related variables such as sexual orientation, aggressiveness and, more controversially, other sex-characteristic traits. Any of these differentiations are taken to be influenced by hormonal effects at specific times, to the exclusion of others. The genetic sex controls the bias towards 'male' or 'female' in regard to all dimensions but overlap, except in the case of genitalia, between 'male' and 'female' distributions is the rule; for example males generally are taller than females, but many females are taller than many males.

Very rarely things go wrong, even in genital development, and genetic sex does not square with external genitalia. What happens to sexual orientation in such cases? Two anomalous conditions are of interest: androgen insensitivity syndrome (AIS), and congenital adrenal hyperplasia (CAH). In the first case we are dealing with genetic males, who, because of a lack of androgen receptor sites, fail to develop morphologically as males. In the most extreme cases the infant will appear to be female and be reared as such. At puberty all the sex characteristics will be female, although menstruation will not occur. Indeed sometimes this is the first clue that something is wrong.

37

From what we know of such case histories, it would appear that they grow up as normal heterosexual females, with no evidence of male-typical behaviour. This could of course be taken as evidence of the power of the environment to shape orientation and other sex-typical behaviours, although it would appear that there are similar genetic conditions in other species which also result in similar behavioural development. In the case of CAH, genetic females are exposed to androgens in male-range quantities during gestation as a result of faulty adrenal gland activity. Even when genital abnormalities are surgically corrected at birth and the children raised as female, it has been reported that over a third of CAH cases show either homosexual or bisexual orientation.

It is too early to come to any firm conclusions about the weighting to be given to neurohormonal factors in determining orientation. Theories which stress their importance (see Ellis and Ames 1987 for a recent review) do make the following salient points. First, since all mammals are fundamentally female unless a Y chromosome initiates masculinization, we would expect all variations in sex-related development, including orientation, to be more common among males. As we have seen, this probably holds true for homosexuality and bisexuality. Second although sexual orientation may be determined separately from other behaviour-related sex differences, it should be the case that some hypothesized hormonal effects will also influence other such differences. With regard to the gay scene, this suggests, perhaps controversially, that effeminate homosexuals may be a sub-set of individuals, in whom a wider range of sexual 'inversions' has pre-natally occurred. On such an issue, I think one would want to keep a good role for the environment too. The final inference we have already considered: if sexual orientation is (largely) determined before birth and involves amongst other things the organization of the subcortical brain, it should be very difficult to modify. It is.

There is often a muddled belief that finding biological causes for variant behaviour makes an 'illness' label for that behaviour more appropriate. This is a dangerous nonsense. There is nothing at all that increases or decreases the probability that anything is an illness. Illnesses are defined by society. By a conference decision — nothing more — the American Psychiatric Association decided not so long ago to remove homosexual orientation from its list of 'illnesses'. That of course does not prevent many people, medically qualified or otherwise, from continuing to see it as such. Left-handedness probably has biological causes: it has also sometimes been seen as an illness, but not because of its origins but because the right-handed majority chose to label it as such.

CONCLUSION

We have identified two major parameters of sexual motivation in humans. The first has to do with what we might term activation: the strength of motivation to indulge in sexual activity of whatever kind. This we take to vary both between individuals and within individuals at any particular time. At a very crude level androgens are 'activators' for both sexes. However human and other primate males will often continue to show, for a time at least, sexual interest after adult castration, whereas the same procedure abolishes sexual activity in rodents. Thus in higher animals generally and man in particular the highly developed cortex can 'manufacture' arousal. Psychologically this is seen in the immensely important role that fantasy can play as perhaps the only genuine aphrodisiac: even erotic pictures tend to cue fantasy involvement. Individual differences in strength of sexual motivation probably reflect differences in people's willingness to expose themselves to internally and externally generated erotic stimulation more than any small differences in levels of hormones, which might anyway be results of sexual arousal rather than causes of it. Differences between the sexes in activation effects are outweighed by similarities.

The second major parameter of sexual motivation has to do with the 'object' of attraction. In the case of males especially this sometimes can encompass, presumably through specific conditioning experiences, great attraction to actual objects. In the main however the objects are persons and these can be either of the opposite sex or the same sex. This parameter is specifically called 'orientation'. There is good evidence that in many males, and probably fewer females, homosexual as well as heterosexual attraction exists. Society's attitudes tend to create pressure to adopt a gay or straight life-style, so substantial bisexuality is probably 'lost' by polarization effects. Exclusive homosexuality does not seem easily predictable by theories which exclusively concentrate on upbringing and/or early sexual experience as determining predominant orientation. Neurohormonal theories, though still speculative with regard to exact mechanisms, seem at least to be plausible in regard to certain kinds of exclusive homosexual orientation. However, while research is so often based on such monumentally flawed sampling procedures (inevitable in the light of societal prejudice) it will be difficult for any firm conclusions to be drawn in this area.

5

Aggression

Most psychologists are rightly wary when they are asked to talk or write about aggression. It is a definitional minefield. We might wish to say that aggression consists of behaviour which is intentionally designed to harm another. Certainly it is hard to avoid including some reference to intention in any definition: a person with bad breath may be guilty of delivering noxious stimuli to those round about but can hardly be accused of aggression. However, surely aggression does not have to be active behaviour? Would it not be aggressive to cause someone harm by failing to inform them of some hazard? What, then, about cheating, malicious gossip, and a host of other indirect means of doing another down? We have to recognize that the word aggression on its own has too wide a potential to serve as much more than what it is in this book: a heading, an umbrella term to cover an array of sub-topics.

The sub-topic which dominates much contemporary popular debate can baldly be called 'violence'. People often seem unconcerned about indirect expressions of aggressive behaviour in such areas as public life, business, the City; at most there may be murmurings about lowered ethical standards, whereby one person's gains and another's losses are brought about by dubious means. However there is often near hysteria about the apparent increase in unsanctioned direct physical aggression, which is a rough definition of violence. What would a Martian make of those primitive displays of punching and kicking which much of the public see as increasing in frequency in our daily lives?

Our Martian, new to the task of observation and taking nothing for granted, tells us of its amazing discovery that the perpetrators and victims of this primitive exercise of aggression are very likely male adolescents from poor backgrounds. We are also informed that episodes of physical violence are of very different kinds: fights with several combatants in which injuries tend not to be very severe (although that cannot be guaranteed), which are nevertheless very noisily conducted; fights between two combatants only, where one at least seems to be in the grip of what earthlings call anger (the injuries here can be much more serious); finally there are those instances where the violence to a person often seems to be merely instrumental in obtaining something like a wallet or a handbag — this category is called by the earthlings 'mugging'.

Many psychologists would be disposed to ask what the pay-off is for certain activities and then assume that frequency of behaviour will relate to pay-off. The Martian's triple division might serve such an approach well. In the first category something to do with group *mores* might provide the clue to the pay-off. Giving way to emotion seems to be involved in the second case. Money might be the beginning and end of the matter in the third case. We shall come back to the role of reward and punishment at a later point, but meanwhile our sexless Martian has made yet another striking observation, namely that aggressive disturbances are also linked to the growing pains of adolescent males in some of our phylogenetically closest relatives, the primates. What role might then be played by biological factors in determining the pattern of aggressive behaviour in human beings? Are males, for example, naturally more inclined to aggression than females?

AGGRESSION IN NON-HUMAN PRIMATES

Ethologists who have studied aggression in non-human primates have variously embraced a concept which has now filtered through to a wider public, that is, the concept of a dominance hierarchy, or, from its origins in the study of domestic fowl, a pecking order. Such a concept is meant as a parsimonious explanation both of who is likely to be aggressive against whom in a social group, and of a certain cohesion which inhibits any frequent incidence of aggression. This latter point is important since in the past some theorists attacked the notion of dominance hierarchies on the grounds that most instances of such patterned aggression were found in animals kept in varying degrees of captivity, and thus such hierarchies might be a mere artefact of such artificial environments. What is true is that animals in zoos are often kept in closer proximity than is normal, and encroachments on personal space encourages aggression. Limited space also makes de-escalation by escape more difficult. However it is perfectly possible to see dominance hierarchies as natural social phenomena designed in normal circumstances to keep the peace, but which are frequently strained to breaking point in the confined environments of captivity.

A more pertinent question to ask is whether the idea of one animal always being dominant over another in all contexts — feeding, mating, etc. — fits the known facts. It is certainly true that dominance ranking should not be seen as an inflexible attribute of an individual on a par with its physical appearance. Who's who in a pecking order can depend on how many 'whos' are present: primates are not beyond forming alliances and coalitions. But when it comes to any two animals it is very often simply the case that 'A consistently bosses B' (Meller 1982). Dominance, however, is, as we have hinted above, not to be thought of as synonymous with aggression. The most dominant animal may well show the least aggression, since he is shown automatic subservience. Thus once a dominance hierarchy is established it tends to decrease levels of aggression in the group. As we might expect, aggression is highest when hierarchies are being formed or when they are disrupted, for example by introducing a new animal into the group.

In the primate species which show most evidence of dominance hierarchies, it is usual for aggression to increase as young males reach puberty and become sexually active. Obviously this could be seen as an easy parallel with the associated aggression, youth, and maleness in the human species, which was mentioned earlier. It is certainly true that something akin to the formation of dominance hierarchies can be seen in adolescent boys. Savin-Williams (1977) studied the behaviour of boys attending a summer camp, and was able to rank the individuals into a dominance hierarchy on the basis of physical and verbal aggression and number of orders given as against number obeyed. As we might expect, most of the aggressive encounters occurred in the first three days of the thirty-five-day study.

It may be true that male humans, like other male primates, are more aggressive than females — this is after all one of the least disputed of all sex differences (see Maccoby and Jacklin 1974) — and that something akin to dominance hierarchies are shown by young human males, at least at the pre-monogamous but sexually active stage when roaming in groups is the norm. But it must also be remembered that cross-culturally the patterns of aggression are by no means invariable in human societies, and leave plenty of scope for levels of aggression and its means of expression to reflect the mores and presumably at some stage the needs of a particular society. It is interesting that the 'need' for strict dominance hierarchies within different primate species seems to differ according to social structures: terrestrial species gathered in large groups with many sexually active males, such as baboons and macaques, usually show evidence of hierarchies; contrarily, arboreal monogamous species such as gibbons show no such obvious pattern.

Displays of aggression, threats, and withdrawal from direct physical aggression, and hierarchical patterns of dominance are embedded in systems of rules that shape, even in infra-human species, highly organized societies, or in the case of teenage gangs, sub-cultures. We should therefore be wary of over-simplistic attempts to find the roots of aggression in biological factors such as hormones. While it is true that primate aggression increases amongst males when sexual competition arises (puberty, peak periods of female receptivity) there seems to be no primitively laid down causal link, for example, between levels of the male hormone testosterone and aggressiveness, although correlation is often reported. There is indeed more evidence from primate studies to suggest that changes in the level of sex and other hormones are a consequence of competitive rivalry and position in dominance hierarchies (Meller 1982). In the case of humans, if we wish to find biological predispositions to violence — the aggressive 'problem' we initially defined — we would be better occupied exploring broad personality genotypes which, though they might not cause aggression, may influence the probability of aggressive responding. For example, being impulsive might mean a greater predisposition to misjudge or break the rules that normally contain aggression. Being less fearful might also mean that injurious consequences to oneself are less effective constraints. The extent to which such personality traits have innate neurophysiological under-pinnings is itself of course a matter of debate. In any event the way these traits exert influence is very often governed by strict rules.

VIOLENCE: THE RULES OF THE GAME

Violence, practised largely but not exclusively by young males, is a social phenomenon. Its recent study on this side of the Atlantic has therefore been strongly influenced by the new European social psychology associated with, amongst others, Rom Harre. A central strand of this approach is that studying behaviour without taking account of its meaning is a fundamentally flawed activity. With regard to the study of aggression and violence, for example, proponents of this approach would not wish to draw too many conclusions from the early social psychology experiments of Bandura and others which showed that exposure to models hitting dolls caused children to do more doll-hitting themselves. Had the children been made more violent? It all depends on the meanings given to actions.

Marsh (1982) has particularly emphasized the distinction that needs to be made between what young males might say about what they do and what they in fact do, in matters of violent behaviour. This is more than just a routine caveat, since the 'rhetorics' are actually an important aspect of the total meaning given to violence by the social group. There is an implicit agreement in the violent sub-culture that reality is to be transformed by distortion and exaggeration, so as to provide an exciting contrast with approved (but for its members unproductive) avenues of gratification through school or work. There is, then, more talk about violence than there is real violence. However there are rules which govern the amount of exaggeration that is allowable before a group member is accused of 'bullshit'. This is not to deny that violence does occur. It is merely to point out that a very false picture might emerge if an edifice of research were to be built on mere self-report data, especially where an intruding researcher might well provide a suitable audience for a good deal of exaggeration and distortion.

ANGER VERSUS INSTRUMENTAL AGGRESSION

This is a distinction which many theorists (for example, Zillman 1979) see as very important when talking about the role of different factors in facilitating or inhibiting the direct expression of physical aggression. Is the punch or the kick designed to achieve some external reward, or is it motivated by anger? This is not quite the same as asking whether the behaviour is rewarded or not, since it is possible to say that giving way to violence when extremely angry releases tension and in the short term at least makes one feel good: tension reduction then becomes the reward. However it is possible to think of many different sources of external reward for non-angry or instrumental aggression. The cool killing by a Mafia hit-man or the high street mugging of a passer-by are obvious examples of concrete criminal gains being the reward of violence. However, a member of our much mentioned youthful and violent sub-culture may attack someone for fun: what that might well lead to is the fun (and reward) of telling the story to his mates in the bar afterwards, probably with the permitted degree of exaggeration. Notably, the reward is still as externally provided as money, though it is not material. If a group of such hooligans were to attack some unfortunate, fear of social 'punishment' might play as significant a motivating role as seeking peer approval: only a token kick or punch may be needed to maintain credibility.

One type of motivation for violence which does not lie neatly in either the angry or the instrumental category is the violence done purely for fun. This area has more relevance to chapter 8, where sensation-seeking behaviour in relation to arousal theory is discussed. Seeking thrills through violence also gets close to the allied but distinct topics of cruelty and sadism, where parallels with other species break down. It might be possible operantly to shape a rodent mugger; I doubt if one could produce a Nazi torturer. Psychodynamic theorists have undoubtedly done more than experimental psychologists to shed light on this dark area of human motivation (see particularly Fromm 1977).

BIOLOGICAL URGE AND CATHARSIS

Whatever distinction we may make between different kinds of aggression, it is certainly the case that psychologists in the main see aggressive behaviour, like any other behaviour, as ultimately under the control of the environment. The point may still be worth stressing, since the ideas of one early ethologist, Konrad Lorenz, still occasionally receive attention in the wider media. Lorenz believed that aggression in man is part of our biological luggage, as it were, and its expression in some shape or form inevitable. It was for Lorenz instinctive, a term which current motivational theorists find worryingly inexact. Adopting a hydraulic model of motivation, Lorenz saw aggressive 'energy' as building up until it finally spilled out into overt behaviour; if its expression was blocked in one channel it would find some other channel. The theoretically absolute inevitability of aggression in Lorenz's view is perhaps its worst feature: in some of his writings it leads to the curious bathos of talk about the need for football and energetic sports, through which the motivational energy can flow. We do need, however, to consider other social implications of Lorenzian ideas which may still be prevalent: in particular the implication that aggressive urges can be harmlessly released through what is called *catharsis*. Portrayers of fictional violence in the media often appeal to what is in essence a cathartic hypothesis: that exposure to the excitement of fantasy violence leaves the viewers or readers happy, contented, and voided of accumulations of

aggressive energy — in short less prepared to be aggressive themselves.

In what is perhaps the most controversial area of social policy on
which psychologists have been asked to speak, one is inhibited from
saying anything too forcefully. However it is the opinion of this writer
that the evidence for the cathartic view is minimal, but the evidence
for its opposite — that exposure to violence is likely to increase violent
behaviour — is also minimal. In fact the research that has been done
seems to break down into the largely trivial (such as the doll-hitting
type of research mentioned earlier) and the more difficult to interpret
research, which needs a more subtle approach than the campaigners
for or against television violence would wish. It is not proposed to
review this specific area in depth but we can highlight some points
of debate.

First, although catharsis naturally forms part of a crude Lorenzian
view of aggression as instinctive, it is not necessarily so linked. On
the contrary, one view might be that aggressive urges may be triggered
by the environment, but once triggered they will grumble on until
expressed in some way or other: insulted by the boss, man comes
home hours later and kicks cat. Second, we should distinguish between
the cathartic effects which watching a violent film may or may not
have, and informative effects of the violent material: no one disputes
that a tiny handful of people sometimes directly imitates acts of
fictionally portrayed violence. Few responsible people consider this
on its own an argument for censorship, otherwise productions of
Shakespeare on television, much watched by responsible persons,
might suffer.

One of the indirect ways in which exposure to screen violence may
have the opposite of a cathartic effect, that is, may increase the
possibility of real violence, is through the mediation of arousal
(Zillman 1979). If arousal has a blind energizing effect on behaviour
(see chapter 8 for further discussion) and if exposure to media-
portrayed violence causes an increase in arousal, then people who
have watched such material may be more likely to show aggression
afterwards, but only if they find themselves in the presence of aggressive cues, if, for example, such a person leaves the cinema and
encounters some frustration or perceived insult. It should be noted,
however, that this is an inconclusive argument: a heightened state of
arousal due to any other cause, such as watching an erotic movie or
riding a roller coaster, might serve the same purpose. Equally, some
non-aggressive behaviour is in principle just as likely to be cued and
energized. We shall see shortly that there are similarities here with the

role that alcohol may play in the expression of violent behaviour. Meanwhile perhaps this is a suitable point to discuss further the importance of immediate causes of aggressive acts, notwithstanding the longer-term factors such as youth, maleness, social and intellectual deprivation which clearly enhance a general tendency to exhibit violence.

IMMEDIATE FACTORS GOVERNING VIOLENCE

Such factors are among the most important for consideration by those, such as police officers, who are routinely involved in coping with violent incidents (see Evans 1983). Perhaps the most reassuring thing one can say to a worried public is that most people, including occasional perpetrators, experience powerful constraints against the direct physical expression of aggression. Even if we put aside moral principles about how people *ought* to conduct themselves, there is still a powerful residue of fear and anxiety connected with involvement in real violence: fear of injurious retaliation, fear of being caught and punished. This may indeed account for some of the exaggeration, distortion, and rhetoric which we noted is often the reality of violent delinquent groups. Perhaps therefore we ought to ask what factors 'disinhibit' the individual and lower the normal threshold for showing violence.

One obvious factor is alcohol. Walter (1981) examined police intervention in violent domestic disputes. Over 70 per cent were alcohol-related. We also know that violent incidents involving football hooligans are often the result of prior intoxication. What then is the nature of this effect, since alcohol in no way directly increases feelings of hostility? The answer is that alcohol does have a direct effect on fear. Such 'Dutch courage' can be seen as an alcoholic effect in laboratory studies with animals as much as in countless real life incidents. It seems likely therefore that alcohol directly depresses the limbic system structures which normally mediate fear and avoidance (see Gray 1971). Thus when a situation with potential for spilling into violence is encountered, alcohol renders the individual less constrained or worried by the possible self-injurious consequences of his actions. It may also be added that the individual in his alcoholic haze will be less cognitively equipped to work out the consequences.

Note that the lowered motivation from fear characteristic of inebriated persons results in a higher likelihood of aggression only when situational cues eliciting aggression are present. This dependency

47

on cues is similar then to the case with arousal mentioned above. Thus in other situations the drunk may be more disposed to be merry, or amorous though impotent, or he may just fall asleep. Lowered fear will however lead to a certain recklessness in all activities: for instance he may fall asleep in the road.

Our primary observation that much violent behaviour occurs when individuals, usually young males, get together in groups prompts us to mention the group itself as a disinhibitory influence with respect to aggression. At least two reasons for this can be given. First, fear motivation is again diminished when battle is conjointly engaged: the individual is likely to feel more secure as a member of a group. Second, personal responsibility is diluted, and the individual feels less of an individual. Social motives involving obedience and conformity to group mores leave little room for personal ethics. The work of psychologists such as Zimbardo on this process of 'deindividuation' is relevant here. Individuals, once they have merged themselves into a mob with corporate identity, can be capable of acts of great violence and cruelty. This becomes the more possible if the shared role is defined by some group uniform: that of a prison guard, a member of the Ku Klux Klan, or a streetwise hooligan wearing the currently dictated fashion.

The extent to which any person would be turned 'monstrous' by the right conditions of deindividuation is a matter of dispute. In one of Zimbardo's classic studies, (Zimbardo 1972) students took the roles of either prisoners or guards in a mock-prison in the basement of a psychology department. The experiment lasted six days, being prematurely halted because of the intensity of brutality and stress engendered in guards and prisoners respectively. The general behaviourist thesis emerging from this study is that perhaps the great majority of people can be made to behave totally out of accord with their own moral standards so long as the situation is compelling enough. This is also the message commonly given most prominence in interpretations of yet another of psychology's most cited experiments: Milgram's (1963) study of obedience, where subjects were requested to deliver what they thought were stronger and stronger electric shocks to a stooge of the experimenter, who played the part of 'learner' in a putative learning experiment. Most subjects obeyed the experimenter's request to carry on giving shocks even after the stooge started kicking the walls, screaming for the experiment to end.

It is certainly true that both experiments will never be replicated: they would nowadays never get past the first meeting of an ethics committee on experimentation. What we can say is that both experiments involved extremely bold manipulation of situational variables. This latter fact, however, has led some critics on close reading of the experimental reports to be most impressed by the extent to which subjects fought against being brutalized by obedience to the experimenters' requirements. In Zimbardo's and Milgram's experiments guards and subjects played their roles obediently, but only a minority showed any signs of sadistically enjoying such moral abandonment. Fromm (1977) reviews both studies in great detail and puts a strong argument against too widespread an acceptance of the behaviourist thesis. The roots of cruelty and destructiveness, for Fromm, lie in disordered personality, not short-term situations. Returning to our discussion of the disinhibiting effects of being in a group, we should be wary of thinking that the individuals concerned are somehow transformed by deindividuation from 'goodies' to 'baddies'; rather, latent aggression linked already to shared *mores* is exaggerated and nearer a threshold of expression when the group comes together.

Neither should we forget the immediate and usually unfortunate role of the 'victim' in cueing an episode of street violence. A suitable target is usually a necessary condition of the violent act. A suitable target may be a member of a rival gang, or a member of a despised minority group (a black, a 'Paki', a gay): residual moral feelings demand that the victim is suitably derogated and dehumanized by belonging to such an out-group. Any behaviour even including not fighting back ('cowardice') can then be used to legitimize further the dehumanization of the victim and therefore the rectitude of the violence. We are reminded of the extremes which such processes have served in the official categorization of Jews as subhumans by the Nazis. It is interesting that even an example of what we previously called purely instrumental violence, namely 'mugging', sometimes also appears to require the derogation of the victim, as if money alone could not fully legitimize the attack. Old people, often the victims, may be seen as a despised group: ominously, as these pages are being written it seems that a somewhat contemptuous collective noun is becoming fashionable to describe old people: 'wrinklies'. Whatever are the harmless uses to which the term may be put, it illustrates well how a collective noun can wonderfully destroy concern with individuality.

To a group with a certain amount of Dutch courage the presence of a suitable victim or two might be enough to precipitate an act of violence. The extent and scope of the violence can however depend on such factors as weapon availability. A famous case of killing in the

USA followed an argument at a game of Bridge, which ended with a wife shooting her husband. One can argue that what would have been a marital 'tiff' in England was transformed by America's liberal gun laws into a violent killing. However some researchers, notably Berkowitz, have gone further and suggested that the presence of weapons can actually help trigger aggression; for example, even being in a room with pictures of guns on the wall will lead to a significantly lower threshold for violence to be expressed following, say, an insult. The methodology of experimentation in this area and many failures to replicate make it difficult to evaluate what must be subtle effects, although theoretically there is nothing particularly puzzling in the notion that affect such as anger might be cued without awareness by certain stimuli. Such emotional effects might then mediate changes in expressed aggression. Another route might be via cognitive priming and selective recall of mood-relevant material (see chapter 10).

Having looked at some of the immediate factors which promote violence, let us now turn to what might be done to reduce it: after all, understanding and controlling phenomena are linked concepts. However the sub-heading which follows is not written without a touch of scepticism.

REDUCING VIOLENCE

The reason for pessimism about the likelihood of any real decrease in violence within our culture, is that there is so much reinforcement for it. With respect to longer term factors, violence still forms an important part of a widely accepted stereotype of approved male behaviour. Heroic male figures are portrayed in the media achieving their 'ends' through violence. No doubt images of the special cop, licensed to commit a little 'aggro' on the side, but all in a good cause, will be seen to reflect reality; they must also reinforce it. Many people rather naïvely believe in making subtle distinctions in legitimizing violence, not realizing that the bloody nose or good hiding advocated by Disgusted of Tunbridge Wells for the treatment of hooligans, is the same remedy advocated by the urban street gang for offenders against their imposed rule in their local territory. The simple truth is that males, be they hooligans or retired majors, are taught to fight for their rights and what they truly believe in. The prevalence of violence within a society takes us beyond the expertise of psychology; it must be looked at in a wider socio-political context. However in the shorter term psychology can tell us something about what can de-escalate individual incidences of violence.

Here we need to reiterate the distinction made earlier between angry and instrumental aggression, since research indicates that different considerations are necessary in dealing with these two types. In the short term the deterrent effect of threat of punishment should not be underestimated, especially with respect to non-angry instrumental violence. We should here distinguish sharply between the meanings of the word 'deterrent' and the word 'corrective'. A deterrent refers to the threat of punishment and its influence on the likelihood of a future transgression. A 'corrective' refers to the effect of actual punishment for a transgression on the likelihood of future transgression. Whereas the evidence is weak that punishment is any kind of corrective, there is a good deal of evidence that threat of punishment can, in the right circumstances, be an excellent deterrent. In that context aggressive responding, when it is not in the immediate service of passionate emotion, can be seen like any other operant behaviour as guided by its consequences. What are the 'right circumstances'? Most importantly, the punishment threatened must be severe enough to be a deterrent, and the likelihood that the punishment will indeed follow the transgression must be high. This simple maxim for creating better law and order would no doubt be endorsed by those frightened members of the public who want to see greater police presence on our streets. The efficacy of probable punishment in inhibiting aggression is confirmed in experimental studies conducted in the laboratory (Baron *et al.* 1974; see Figure 1). Why then is this on its own not enough to reduce the frequency of violent incidences?

First, and with respect to an individual incident of street violence, the probability of being caught is not likely to be high enough to have its full deterrent effect without a truly massive police presence. This is not of course to assert that existing levels of policing are not beneficial, only that they are inadequate. Second, we have stressed that threat of punishment is only really effective against non-angry displays of violence. The findings of Baron *et al.* illustrated in Figure 1 confirm that the effect of punishment threat on angry aggression is non-existent. If therefore the presence of a 'cue' which signalled probability of punishment for transgression — a police officer — were also to arouse anger and other powerful negative emotions then violence may not be inhibited. Clearly training in law enforcement is designed to avoid this; however, police officers are only human and sometimes respond in less than ideal ways. More to the point one cannot talk about the efficacy of a police officer as an upholder of

51

Figure 1 The inhibiting effect of punishment threats (but not on anger-induced aggression)

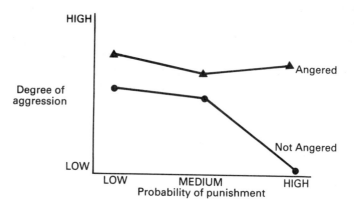

(After Baron *et al.* 1974)

Figure 2 The inhibiting effect of humour (in the case of anger-induced aggression)

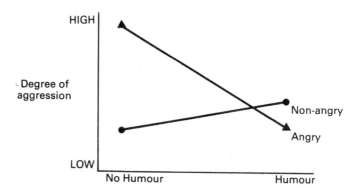

(After Baron *et al.* 1974)

law and order within a community without first noting the context of police-community relations in general.

Angry aggression usually results from some obvious frustration or insult and clearly implies that the aggressor is in a highly aroused emotional state. Research by social psychologists suggests that, in the short term, strategies for reducing actual violence rely on distracting an individual from the source of frustration and anger and allowing arousal to be reduced. Baron *et al*. (1974) showed that humour can often serve to dispel angry aggression (see Figure 2). Longer-term discouragement of aggressiveness depends on how far a culture teaches physical violence as a response to frustration. Frustration and aggression are easily linked — in other species too — but cultural differences suggest that social learning can still drive a wedge between what is essentially feeling and what is essentially behaviour. Human emotions are capable of being dealt with, expressed, coped with, vented, etc., showing a diversity of outcomes far removed from early views that so closely linked frustration and aggression.

CONCLUSION

Aggression is potentially definable as a very wide area of behaviour. We have tended to limit our discussion to primitive displays of physical aggression which are taken as disruptive in the context of a society. Although aggressive encounters and dominance hierarchies in primates were looked at, even these can be seen as illuminating often complex social structures within the groups studied, as also can real life studies of delinquent groups of young human males. Physical violence is not therefore as far as psychological research has shown an inevitable expression of man's biological nature.

There is every reason however to be pessimistic about the continuance of violence in our societies because it is so obviously a source of reward. It is so, especially as part of a desirable male stereotype, itself ironically shared by aggressors in two sub-cultures, those in one wishing to mete out the most violent punishment to those in the other. Both legitimize violence as a means to an end. Progress in the control of undesirable aggression might be furthered by the dispelling of notions that aggression is instinctive and therefore must be expressed by some sort of catharsis. Notwithstanding the chronic roots of societal violence, deterrence is almost certainly an important factor controlling levels of gratuitous, non-angry, unprovoked violent incidences in a community. Distraction, humour, and mood changing strategies generally are the best ways of lowering angry aggression. Being a member of a group and being under the influence of alcohol serve to disinhibit the individual from normal deterrent constraints against violence.

6

Gut reactions and gut emotions

INTRODUCTION

Humankind has lived but a blink of an eye in anything resembling a modern society. Civilization defined by the most liberal criteria is measured in thousands of years, while the lifetime of our species is measured in millions. Thus when our bodies respond to emergencies, we are seeing a pattern of response whose adaptive value must be measured against the survival requirements pertaining to that approximately 99.9 per cent of our time on earth. The autonomic nervous system (ANS) lies at the heart of what the physiologist, Walter Cannon, referred to as emergency motivation. Let us then begin with a brief introduction to the anatomy and physiology of the ANS.

BASIC STRUCTURE AND FUNCTION

The ANS is a branch of the peripheral nervous system, that is, it lies outside the brain and the spinal cord (see Figure 3). It automatically controls the day-to-day activities necessary for our survival. A vast range of variables, from heart rate to insulin level, is regulated according to need. The ANS governs the body's metabolic requirements. Metabolic processes can be seen as dividing into two kinds, broadly speaking: 'anabolic' (concerned with the building up of reserves) and 'catabolic' (concerned with breaking down and converting stored reserves to meet immediate energy demands). These two types of opposing processes are mirrored in the structure of the ANS, which is divided into two branches: the sympathetic and the parasympathetic. The sympathetic is basically catabolic and the parasympathetic basically anabolic. The ANS nerves connect spinal

Figure 3 A simplified schematic diagram showing the main anatomical features of the autonomic nervous system

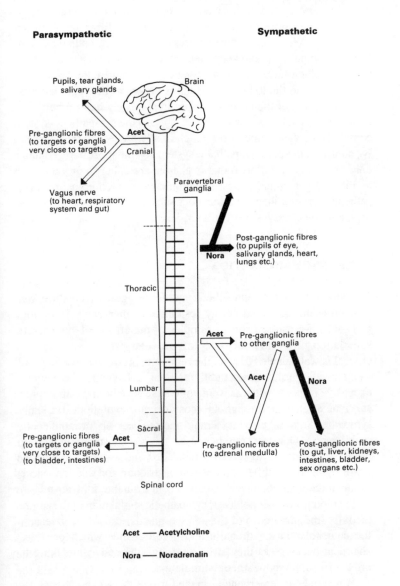

Acet —— Acetylcholine

Nora —— Noradrenalin

cord and various target organs and smooth muscle. Anatomically the sympathetic and parasympathetic divisions are separate (see Figure 3). Sympathetic nerves leave the spinal cord in the central thoracolumbar regions, while the parasympathetic nerves have their outflow from the very top and the very bottom of the spinal cord (craniosacral regions). The figure reveals another anatomical difference between the systems. Whereas the nerve fibres of the parasympathetic system leave the spinal cord and keep themselves relatively separate as they proceed to their target, the sympathetic fibres immediately pass from spinal cord into the long mass which is known as the 'paravertebral ganglia'. Some of the nerves synapse immediately here; others pass on to other ganglia, but with few exceptions the sympathetic system contains post-ganglionic fibres which finally proceed to their targets. By contrast, the parasympathetic system for the most part, contains only pre-ganglionic fibres, that is ganglia are either in or very close to their target. Finally post-ganglionic (thus predominantly sympathetic) nerves utilize the transmitter substance 'noradrenalin', while pre-ganglionic nerves are cholinergic.

EMERGENCY MOTIVATION

The anatomy of the sympathetic system suggests a creature well adapted to an integrated bodily response to emergency. If we look at Table 1 we can see some examples of the effects of sympathetic stimulation on various organs. In particular, general sympathetic arousal is well adapted to meet the requirements of what we may call, using a well-worn phrase, 'fight' or 'flight' behaviour. These energy expensive response patterns would of course have been the appropriate survival strategies throughout most of our evolution. Basically, sympathetic arousal provides a multi-faceted back-up for rapid energy mobilization. Our heart rate increases, oxygen consumption goes up, blood is channelled to where it is needed and away from where it is not by means of differential vaso-constriction and dilation. Stored sugar in the liver is converted into a form available for transmission by the blood. Last but not least, sympathetic stimulation of the adrenal medulla (the inner core of the adrenal glands) causes the release of the catecholamines, adrenalin and noradrenalin, which provide a chemical back-up, as they stream through the body mimicking the effects of direct sympathetic stimulation.

When meeting emergencies in the form of threats, another slower acting neuroendocrine system is also involved, which we may call

Table 1 Some functions of sympathetic and parasympathetic stimulation of target systems

Target system	Sympathetic stimulation	Parasympathetic stimulation
Eye pupil	Dilation	Constriction
Tear gland	—	Secretion
Salivary gland	Scant thick secretion	Profuse watery secretion
Heart rate	Increase	Decrease
Bronchial tubes	Dilation	Constriction
Blood vessels (skin)	Constriction	Dilation
Blood vessels (muscle)	Dilation	Constriction
Stomach motility	Decrease	Increase
Adrenal medulla	Stimulates secretion of catecholamines	—
Sweat glands	Stimulates activity	—

the pituitary-adrenocortical axis. This system was largely ignored by Cannon but received much attention from Hans Selye, who is often seen as the father of modern 'stress' research. The pituitary gland, situated at the base of the brain, is triggered by the hypothalamus, to secrete a substance known as adrenocorticotrophic hormone (ACTH) which stimulates the outer part (corex) of the adrenal glands to produce chemicals known as steroids. There are two major classes of adrenal steroids: mineralocorticoids and glucocorticoids. Extremely diverse in their effects, steroids can nevertheless be seen as yet another back-up in what originally were primitive physical means of coping with emergencies: for example, glucocorticoids are known to be highly influential in promoting muscular efficiency. Normally we may expect that primitive coping with primitive emergencies was a relatively short-term affair, and, indeed, built into the system is a classic negative feedback loop. High levels of circulating steroids serve to turn off production of ACTH by the pituitary. It was left to Selye (1956) to speculate about the implications of living with more modern 'stress', where threats may be psychological, interpersonal, and chronic in nature.

SELYE'S GENERAL ADAPTATION SYNDROME

Selye describes what he calls a General Adaptation Syndrome (GAS), which sees the body as going through three stages of response to stress. First an alarm stage, second a stage of resistance, and third a stage of exhaustion. The relationship between these three stages and the body's ability to cope is diagrammatically represented in Figure 4. The role of the pituitary-adrenocortical axis is an important part of Selye's conceptualization of stress. The longer term effects of steroids are detrimental to health. It is well known that steroids are used in medicine for their very powerful anti-inflammatory properties, but they are also used with great caution. The inflammation response is a necessary part of the body's healing processes. Other inimical effects of steroids include immunosuppression, so lowering the body's resistance to infection. Thus a failure to cope, or, what amounts to the same thing, a constant need to reactivate coping to counteract a persistent threat, we would expect to lead to illness and *in extremis* exhaustion and death.

The details of Selye's case for a GAS, general across species and

Figure 4 Selye's General Adaptation Syndrome.
Closed line illustrates specific coping with a particular stressor. Hatched line illustrates ability to cope with other stressors.

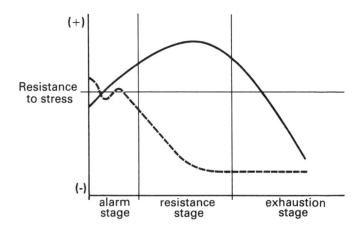

across stressors, have not gone without criticism. For example it is very difficult to be clear about the general physiological effects of physical stressors such as heat, cold, physical injury, or anything else, since specific effects will cloud the picture. There are those, notably Mason (1971), who would argue that GAS effects are essentially reactions to psychological stress, and reflect such factors as the availability and effortfulness of coping strategies. Nevertheless Selye's ideas, with refinement, still lie at the heart of that area of psychosomatics concerned with the relationship between stress and illness.

For more detailed coverage of the physiology of this area the reader should consult more specialized texts (for example, Van Toller 1979; Cox 1979; Cooper 1983). In motivational terms, however, we can see how the notion of emergency motivation encapsulates well an integrated bodily response to threatening circumstances. We need, though, in our more modern world, to be flexible in our interpretation of emergency. Out on the savannah our ancestors would no doubt have considered the close presence of a large and hungry carnivore a definite emergency. No doubt the emergency would involve strong feelings of emotion as well — a major point we are about to take up. However emergencies can be seen as lying at the end of a continuum which we could label: 'things which we are required to deal with'. It would be strange then if our body's responses did not also reflect the existence of such a continuum. We may therefore expect ANS arousal — at less dramatic levels perhaps — to reflect the day-to-day effort and coping that we put into meeting much more mundane challenges, even such as solving problems in a psychologist's laboratory. This is indeed the case and the reader is referred to chapter 7 for instances of psychophysiological research in relation to coping.

THE ROLE OF THE ANS IN EMOTION

All of us who have just had a near miss while driving a car, or a good portion of the population who may have encountered a large hairy spider in the bath tub will have noticed a concomitance of acute emotion and bodily sensations such as a pounding heart and sweaty hands. Such nasty shocks are associated with ANS activity. The question arises whether the ANS activity is a core part of the experience of emotion.

At the end of the last century two theorists, William James and Carl Lange, both independently suggested that autonomic feedback was indeed an essential ingredient in emotional experience. The fact that we often talk about emotions such as fear and anger as 'gut' emotions may lead us to view these theories as plausible. Lange, in 1885, put forward his theory in a robust form which has the virtue at least of being eminently testable. He believed that the entire emotional side of experience was due to the reactions of our vasomotor system. It, and it alone, gave emotional quality to our mental life. Without it we would wander through life 'passionless'. To what extent has the James-Lange theory of emotion been supported by experimental testing? We shall review the evidence, but the reader will *en route* find out a pervasive truth: that testing theories of emotion is never as clear-cut as it seems.

One obvious research strategy is to see what happens when the crucial ANS feedback is removed. Since the reactions we are considering involve sympathetic 'arousal', it is possible to make use of techniques which destroy the sympathetic nervous system, that is, sympathectomy. Unlike the parasympathetic system, the sympathetic branch can be totally destroyed without causing death. Cannon *et al.* (1927) were among the first to conduct experiments in this area. They reported that sympathectomized cats showed no emotional deficiencies when exposed to a naturalistic threat in the form of fierce dogs. Cannon took this to be an important refutation of a James-Lange type of theory. However we may well demur in this regard. Cannon was only reporting on the behaviour of the animal. Short of asking his cats whether the quality of their experience had changed, Cannon could not comment on James-Lange as a theory of emotional experience. It is perfectly possible to assert that the cat's emotional reactions were simply well learned patterns of response to suitable stimuli. This is of course tantamount to saying that animal experiments must in the end be largely irrelevant to testing the issue at hand. This is in fact the case. However even in the animal laboratory, the findings are not so totally ranged against a weaker form of James-Lange theory.

Studies of avoidance conditioning (where an animal learns to make a response in the presence of a warning stimulus to avoid the receipt of a noxious stimulus) have often been conducted to test a so-called 'two-factor' theory of avoidance. This theory in its strongest form suggests that successful avoidance is achieved by a combination of two learning processes — hence the name. First, conditioned emotional responses are by Pavlovian means elicited by the warning stimulus. Second, these emotional responses are felt as aversive and an avoidance response is learned by operant means which successfully gets the animal out of the 'fearful' situation. Since emotional processes are assumed to play a crucial mediating role in learning such responses, we would expect, if James-Lange were correct, that removal of sympathetic activity, either through surgical intervention or pharmacological blockade, would prevent successful avoidance responses being acquired. It does not.

However the results can be taken as giving some support for a weaker form of James-Lange theory. Conditioned emotional responses do play a role in avoidance behaviour (see Mineka 1979), but avoidance learning is certainly not prevented by removal of sympathetic responding. Just as thirty or more years of experimentation have not killed off all forms of two-factor avoidance theory (Boyd and Levis 1983), they have not permitted the total dismissal of James-Lange either. But here we may return to our original point. Animal experimentation can have no bearing on experiential aspects of the theory. What about human studies?

The clouds surrounding individuals sometimes provide silver linings for researchers. It is possible to ask whether any lessening of emotional experience follows unfortunate accidents involving transection of the spinal cord. Anecdotal evidence from the early part of this century suggested that no change in capacity for feeling intense emotions occurred. But such conclusions were based on physicians' impressions. More recently Hohmann (1966), himself a paraplegic, conducted a survey among spinal injury patients and found that they did report a diminution in the intensity of their emotions. One said that the heat had gone out of the emotion, that anger was a kind of 'mental' anger. More recently still, however, Lowe and Carroll (1985) have repeated Hohmann's study and found no evidence for a diminution of feeling in paraplegics. Why the difference? Perhaps Hohmann's position as a paraplegic himself allowed him to be more sensitive to picking up the evidence of emotional change. However, it is equally possible that spinal injury patients had, two decades ago, different expectations about the effects of their injuries. Suggestion and expectation effects are at their strongest in this kind of research strategy, based as it is so crucially on retrospective recall and comparison of present and past states.

Cannon, the great critic of James-Lange, had other criticisms to marshal against the theory. The ANS was too slow a beast to play the role required of it. This is essentially an appeal to the court of common experience: have we not all experienced instant emotions before our innards start churning? However, even if this point is allowed, it does not tell against a weaker form of James-Lange which states, for example, that the ANS fills in, as it were, the essential depth to the emotional experience. This line of argument suggests a theme which we shall pursue in a later chapter more specifically concerned with cognition and emotion: it may be helpful to distinguish between primary and secondary types of emotion.

Another criticism by Cannon concerned the specific nature of different emotions. It was not possible, thought Cannon, to point to different patterns of visceral activity associated with different emotions. With respect to the gutsy emotions of fear and anger, Cannon may be wrong on this point.

Ax (1953) reported results from an experiment the current importance of which rests on his bold, and to modern eyes unethical, manipulation of emotional states. Convincingly he persuaded subjects, wired up with recording electrodes, that they were in mortal danger of electrocution from faulty apparatus. Alternatively they were roundly insulted by a 'stooge' of the experimenter. There can be little doubt that Ax reliably produced in his subjects the emotions of fear and anger respectively. Ax went on to show that these different emotions were accompanied by different patterns of peripheral physiological activity. Since then it has become clear that the pattern of activity associated with fear is one in which the catecholamine, adrenalin, is dominant, whereas anger leads to a greater involvement of noradrenalin.

However, even if the James-Lange theory were to confine its attention to these primitive emotions, it remains unclear whether these different patterns of activity have a direct bearing on perception of emotional state. From an evolutionary standpoint the emotion of anger would be allied to fighting and the emotion of fear to flight. Physiological differentiation may have more to do with maximizing the efficiency of related behavioural responses than with emotions *per se*. Indeed Ax argued that successful fighting requires greater organization of bodily functioning. Frankenhaeuser (1980) has reported on many years of research at the University of Stockholm which suggests that noradrenalin involvement in physiological response to challenge increases when greater activity is required.

Quite apart from difficulties in interpreting the evidence of physiological differentiation for even these two primary emotions, there is, as Cannon also noted, a difficulty for James-Lange in terms of how persons themselves make the necessary discriminations on the basis of autonomic feedback. What the psychophysiologist records the person does not necessarily register. Although biofeedback studies have provided some evidence that visceral perception is possible (Brener 1983), there is also an abundance of evidence suggesting that ability to make routine fine discriminations of visceral feedback is not well developed.

If we try to reach some sort of conclusion on the evidence put forward so far it would have to be that emotion involves more than just the visceral feedback envisaged by James and Lange. On the other hand there is sufficient latitude of interpretation allowed by the studies presented to hold the view that in the normal individual with an intact ANS visceral feedback, albeit of a relatively undifferentiated kind, may be an important input in determining felt emotion. Other inputs however must be considered and if we are to take the view that emotion is a more complex matter we must at the physiological level follow Cannon in searching for central nervous system mechanisms underpinning it, mechanisms which enable higher cognitive processes from cortical inputs to be integrated into the full expression of emotion. A detailed coverage, however, of physiology and emotion in terms of the central nervous system is beyond the scope of this text and the interested reader should consult one of the many specialized texts on physiological psychology.

Cannon himself believed that the thalamus played a vital role in determining full emotional expression. Bard and Mountcastle (1948) showed that if the brain of a cat were transected at the level of the thalamus, the animal no longer seemed to react with true emotional rage when presented with a suitable stimulus. Instead the animal showed a very brief so-called 'sham rage' which lasted only as long as the stimulus was around. Removal of the stimulus switched off the reaction as if it were just a collection of automatic reflexes. The thalamic Cannon-Bard theory reflected only part of the growing experimental findings which related emotion to a great number of central nervous system structures. The work of Papez (1937) and MacLean (1949) pointed to the wider importance of those subcortical areas of the brain: the limbic system. With regard to hedonic theories of reward and punishment, in turn linked to behavioural approach and avoidance, contemporary neuroscientists have continued to stress involvement of hypothalamic and limbic system structures in their theories. In chapter 8 we discuss, for example, the relevance of Gray's (1971) theory to arousal and sensation-seeking behaviour (Zuckerman 1979). So-called 'pleasure' and 'punishment' centres have been discovered in these areas which in animals lead to vigorous barpressing to switch stimulation on or off respectively (Olds 1956; Roberts 1958). As regards emotional experience, the little we know from those ethically permitted instances where stimulation has taken place in human beings, as part of a medical procedure, such stimulation is accompanied by strong pleasurable or unpleasurable emotion.

TOWARDS COGNITION

The drift of the evidence suggests that peripheral feedback from the ANS may play some role in determining emotional experience, but not the only role, and perhaps not even a necessary one. In addition it is likely that such feedback is interpreted in a relatively undifferentiated way as visceral 'arousal'. The idea that higher cognitive processes are responsible for labelling that arousal as a specific emotion constitutes the core of the cognitive-physiological theory put forward by Stanley Schachter.

Schachter and Singer (1962) reported the results of an experiment, which is certainly among the most cited in the whole of psychology. Given its citation pre-eminence, it is as well to consider the experiment's design characteristics in some detail. Table 2 presents a schematic outline of the design. In essence, subjects were randomly assigned to one of seven conditions. Four conditions involved a subject being in the presence of a confederate of the experimenter who behaved in a 'euphoric' fashion. Three conditions involved an 'angry' confederate. The four 'euphoric' conditions break down as follows: 1) subjects received an injection of adrenalin and were informed about its likely physiological effects: 'What will probably happen is that your hand will start to shake, your heart will start to pound, and your face may get warm and flushed.' 2) Subjects were given adrenalin but were left ignorant of effects: the subject were told 'The injection is mild and harmless and will have no side effects.' 3) Subjects were given adrenalin and misinformed about its effects: 'What will probably happen is that your feet will feel numb, you will have an itching sensation over parts of your body, and you may get a slight headache.' 4) Subjects received a placebo injection of saline, which has no physiological effects, nor were subjects told to expect any. The three 'angry' conditions repeated the 'euphoric' ones but without the misinformed condition.

All subjects were given the same 'cover story' which kept them ignorant of the true purpose of the experiment. The injections were supposedly of a vitamin substance. The purported aim of the experiment was to investigate the effects of the injection on vision. After the injection subjects were led to believe that the vitamin took twenty minutes to get into the bloodstream and during this time they were to wait with the confederate, described as another volunteer, in the room. The experimenter apologized for the chaotic state of the room, since there had not been time for a clean-up. This allowed certain 'props' to be lying about which were used by the confederate in his

Table 2 A summary of the design and principal results of Schachter and Singer (1962)

	Drug conditions Adrenalin informed	Adrenalin uninformed	Adrenalin misinformed	Placebo
Euphoria conditions	a, b A	a	b A	
Anger conditions	C	C D	(condition not run)	D

Shared letters indicate statistically significant comparisons. Lower case refers to self-report measure, upper case to behavioural measure. In all cases, comparisons indicate less mood manipulation in 'adrenalin informed' and/or 'placebo' conditions.

acting out the euphoric role. Subjects in the 'euphoric' conditions were treated to a display of happy high jinks on the part of the confederate during the waiting period, including playing 'basket ball' with crumpled paper, shooting paper darts, and ending with hoola-hoop antics, activities in which the subjects were invited to participate. In the 'angry' conditions, subject and confederate were given highly personal and intrusive questionnaires to fill in which the confederate pretended to find offensive and to which he reacted with increasing rage, ending up by stamping out of the room.

So much for the procedure. What did Schachter and Singer expect to find out and what did they find out? They argued that an emotion is jointly determined by physiological arousal and cognitions determined by the social context in which the arousal is felt. Thus they hypothesized that arousal would be treated as non-emotional if the subject had received correct instructions about the effects of adrenalin. If the subjects were left ignorant of the effects of adrenalin, or were misinformed, they would experience unaccountable arousal which they would seek to label according to the context provided by the confederate. Finally if physiological arousal was not induced (the placebo condition) cognitions concerning social context would not on their own produce emotion.

Schachter and Singer, in their write-up, claimed to have largely supported these hypotheses. After the experiment subjects in the 'euphoric' condition reported greater happiness ratings if they were ignorant or misinformed about the effects of adrenalin. In addition, their behaviour, as observed through a one-way mirror, showed greater euphoria and joining in with the antics of the confederate. In the anger condition, Schachter and Singer found problems with the subjects' willingness to report negative emotions to the 'authority' figure of the experimenter, since that figure had been the target for hostile emotion. However the behavioural observation indices were in line with prediction.

On closer examination there are difficulties with the interpretation of Schachter and Singer's results. First of all, the crucial measure of physiological arousal was crude: they took a single measure of pulse-rate before and after the experiment. Psychophysiologists would nowadays prefer more than a single measure and would look for more continuous monitoring, though it should be said that pulse-rate was consistent with differential arousal between adrenalin and placebo groups. More important, the effects found were not large effects, and were in some important comparisons either non-significant statistically or only marginally so. Placebo groups did not show significantly less emotion than adrenalin-ignorant or adrenalin-misinformed groups. The largest difference was between adrenalin-informed and adrenalin-misinformed: the misinformed group reported themselves twice as happy after the experiment as the informed group. However in terms of the scales used to measure self-report the absolute magnitude of difference does not seem great.

Schachter and Singer carried out *post-hoc* adjustments to their comparisons, in order to try to counter the force of some of these criticisms. They argued, for example, that placebo subjects to some extent may have become physiologically aroused without any drug mediation and would therefore show more emotion than those who had clear instructional cues to attribute arousal to the effects of a (genuinely) arousing drug; unfortunately the experimenters did not manipulate instructions among those receiving a placebo, so we cannot directly compare two subject groups both of which are given a placebo but one of which is (falsely) instructed to expect bodily symptoms of arousal. However the authors did show that the crucial comparisons in their experiment were improved by taking account of the 'real' arousal levels of the subjects, as determined by pulse-rate data.

The less than clear-cut picture that emerges from this celebrated study has not been totally resolved since. There have been replications (Erdman and Janke 1978) which broadly agree with the central tenet of Schachter's theory: that physiological and cognitive factors combined to produce emotional experience. But there have also been difficulties, notably a number of researchers have found that a general negative emotional state tends to follow injections of genuinely autonomic-arousing drugs, especially when subjects are uninstructed with regard to effects. Dose factors, and timing factors interacting with individual differences could easily play havoc with any simple view about whether in any instance a subject attributes their arousal to an emotional or non-emotional source. At this point we may wish to conclude that the methodology of this sort of experiment is, despite its original ingenuity, likely to be forever flawed.

Whatever else Schachter and Singer demonstrated, they certainly showed the importance of cognition and social context in determining emotion. The ambiguity concerns the position of autonomic arousal on a continuum of importance. We have seen it downgraded from its pre-eminence in the theories of James and Lange. In the rise of the more thorough-going cognitive theories of emotion which followed Schachter's own theory, we shall see how psychologists have questioned whether autonomic processes have any necessary role at all. Might emotions be simply cognitions? Such questions we leave to chapter 10 of the book.

CONCLUSION

The involvement of the ANS in the experience of primary emotional states, such as fear and anger, has been a major area of investigation during the entire century. Early theories of James and Lange stressed the importance of ANS feedback as a necessary condition for the experience of an emotion. A succinct critique of such theories was published by Cannon which offered a number of discrediting lines of evidence. Recent evidence however is less clear-cut with regard to a number of Cannon's objections. Schachter's theory of emotions, which stresses the interplay of cognitive social and physiological factors, while having been extremely influential in recent years, is seen to have considerably less empirical support than is sometimes supposed. Further discussion of the 'cognitivization' of emotion is left to the final chapter of this book.

7

Predicting and controlling

INTRODUCTION

Those psychologists who have spent the best part of this century investigating the bar-pressing behaviour of white rats and the key-pecking behaviour of pigeons have invariably written a very tangible carrot or stick into their experimental settings. However some of the most interesting work to come out of the operant laboratories concerns not so much the way in which food rewards and electric shock punishments directly control behaviour but rather how signals (in the form of lights, bells, and buzzers) control an animal's responding. For those interested in human motivation the analogy is clear. Our everyday actions are governed, as Rachlin (1976) puts it, by such things as clocks and calendars, bank statements and balances.

In this chapter we explore initially that area of operant research which is variously called 'secondary' or 'acquired' reinforcement. We shall first of all consider how simple stimuli such as lights can come to exercise powerful control over behaviour through their 'association' (leaving that word vague for now) with primary events like food delivery. We shall see that theories to account for such behaviour even in pigeons and white rats need to consider 'motives', which are not unrelated to what taxonomists of human motivation characteristically term 'mastery' motives. In short we shall discover that right across the species that variously trace our evolutionary inheritance, psychologists have found evidence that individuals (rat or undergraduate) seek predictability and controllability in the worlds that they inhabit. We shall see that in the case of man at least his extraordinary sense of space and time interacts with such motives to produce some special twists and turns. In particular human subjects may often find themselves in situations where they would rather staunch the flow of information, than encourage it. In the sea of rewarding and punishing events that constitutes life, information is something that has to be handled, has to be coped with. An examination of this coping and how it affects the individual (in body as well as in mind) will be the concern of the second half of this chapter.

THEORIES OF SECONDARY REINFORCEMENT

Early days

It may seem strange that early theories of secondary reinforcement would have predicted that we would turn off the weatherman on television because of his constant association with aversive events. And yet this would, with a bit of tongue in cheek, have been the case.

When conditioning theories were at their simplest it was assumed that stimuli encountered in close proximity and just prior to a primary reinforcing or punishing event came to exhibit the same properties as the primary event. This was thought to be due to a Pavlovian process whereby the secondary stimuli came to 'substitute' as it were for the primary.

Superficially there was evidence of a sort for such a view. Rats who had been trained to press a bar in a Skinner box for a food reward preceded by a momentary click from the apparatus were found to continue bar-pressing longer, when food was withheld, if they still continued to receive the click. In conditioning parlance the click delayed extinction (Bugelski 1938). Similarly, animals could be shown to learn new operant responses in new situations in order to obtain these so-called 'secondary' reinforcers. Equally it could be demonstrated that stimuli which were closely associated with an aversive event such as an electric shock came to elicit fear in their own right, and that in some circumstances an animal would learn a new response in order to terminate such a stimulus. Thus it was tempting to conclude that these previously neutral stimuli — lights, tones, etc. — had picked up reinforcing or punishing properties in their own right by a kind of 'rub-off' principle, rather as a nail can be turned into a magnet by stroking it against a primary magnet.

It is one thing to conclude that stimuli habitually encountered in close contiguity with a primary 'emotive' event will come to elicit at least emotional twinges in their own right. There is indeed plenty of evidence for the existence of conditioned emotional responses,

69

especially in the literature dealing with aversive and frustrating events. However it is quite another thing to insist that such stimuli behave exactly as substitutes in terms of reinforcing and motivating properties.

An experiment by Schuster (1969) is sufficient of itself to illustrate how the more naïve predictions of the 'rub-off' theory are given short shrift by key-pecking pigeons. Schuster allowed his pigeons to make an operant response which let them choose between two conditions of food reward — known as a concurrent chain procedure. One option was to receive food and a stimulus reliably paired with it. The alternative option was identical except that additional presentations of the stimulus were given even when no food was forthcoming. If by association with the food the stimulus becomes reinforcing in its own right, then it stands to reason that the second option is much the more preferable, for it enables the pigeon to receive more re-inforcement *in toto*: primary reinforcement is added to by secondary. The pigeons however thought better of it and showed a marked preference for the first option. Why? Rachlin (1976) rightly points out that asking the pigeon to prefer the second option is like asking a hotel guest to prefer a hotel which sounds its dinner gong at all hours of the day as well as prior to dinner. Such a hotel might generate more gallons of saliva from its guests but will not necessarily be preferred.

Indeed secondary reinforcers do have effects which are of considerable interest to the student of motivation, even though they are not strictly speaking reinforcing. One of the obvious uses of secondary reinforcers is that they can bridge a delay between responding and primary reinforcement. Thus in a celebrated study by Wolfe (1936) chimpanzees learned to press a lever for a poker chip which could be used at a later time in a slot machine to buy a grape. It is clear in a general way that neutral stimuli reliably paired with primary reinforcement become as it were 'promissory notes', just like bank notes. When the promise is lost, however, as it was in the great German inflation of the 1920s, the notes will lose their magnetism in a way that the aforementioned nail does not.

As long as some connection with primary reinforcement is maintained, secondary reinforcers do have genuine motivational characteristics. In the Schuster experiment reported above, although the pigeons did not show a preference for the condition giving extra secondary reinforcers, they did in another study demonstrate a faster rate of responding in that condition. This is typical also of what are called second-order schedules of reinforcement, a term in need of explanation.

Suppose we arrange that a pigeon has to peck a key one hundred times to earn a food delivery. The pigeon is said to be on a fixed ratio 100 schedule. However, reality is what we construct and define. There is no law which tells us to define a response unit as a single key peck. Let us be more molar and define a response as ten key pecks. Let us signal to the pigeon by briefly flashing a light when ten key pecks have been achieved. Finally let us give the pigeon a reward when ten of these more molar responses have been made. In the sense that the pigeon has still to make ten times ten (i.e. a hundred) pecks, it may appear that the situation is identical to fixed ratio 100, although we call this a second order schedule in which a fixed ratio 10 component schedule has to be executed ten times.

Of course in terms of number of key pecks needed to earn food the two situations are indeed identical. The only observable difference is that in one condition food delivery is reliable preceded by ten 'staging' signals. The effect of these extra signals is to increase the rate of responding in this condition — a finding which mirrors Schuster's results, and may not be entirely irrelevant to the applied psychologist with an interest in marketing. If you wanted to promote a product by giving away prizes for so many wrappers, it might be worth including valueless staging posts, especially if many wrappers are required per prize. Thus ten wrappers might produce an ostensibly useless paper certificate and ten certificates might earn the buyer a prize.

An interesting aspect to this case is that the signals associated with primary reward do not have to be absolutely contiguous with it. They simply reliably precede it. This observation provided a natural link to more plausible theories of secondary reinforcement effects.

Informativeness theories

It has been suggested that one condition necessary for the establishment of a secondary reinforcer is that the stimulus should provide information about when primary reinforcement is due. Such a theory does indeed get support from a number of classic experiments.

Egger and Miller (1962) paired food reward with two signalling stimuli. In one condition of the experiment signal A appeared momentarily before signal B; food followed. Although signal B's onset was closer in time to the presentation of food, it was also, from an informativeness point of view, completely redundant. A rat wanting to know when reinforcement was due would know immediately on

71

receipt of signal A. In the second condition of the experiment it was arranged that signal A would also occur on its own at other times as well as just at food presentations. Thus although signal A was a necessary condition of food, it was not sufficient. Signal B, however, was kept necessary and sufficient as a condition: its presence guaranteed food; food in its absence was not forthcoming. When Egger and Miller later gave rats the opportunity to press a bar to get the signals — a routine test of secondary reinforcement potential — the rats chose to press more for signal A following exposure to the first condition of the experiment, but more for signal B following the second condition. Thus rats preferred whichever signal was the more informative. Clearly more than passive association processes were at work.

In an experiment by Bower *et al.* (1966), we see further evidence that organisms prefer situations which are informative to those which are not. The important aspect of this experiment is that the amount of primary reward available in the two conditions of the experiment is identical. Pigeons were able to make an operant response, as in the Schuster experiment, which gave them access to either of the conditions. In both conditions food was delivered either on a fixed interval 40 seconds schedule or a fixed interval 10 seconds schedule. In both conditions it was randomly determined which schedule was in operation at any one time. What then was the difference between the two conditions given that they offered identical earnings schemes? The answer lies in the colours of the keys. In one condition the key remained yellow throughout. In the other condition the key was red if FI40s was operative and green if the schedule was FI10s. Although the pigeons gained no extra reward from choosing the informativeness condition they nevertheless did choose it, suggesting that informativeness itself was reinforcing.

It might seem tempting to conclude that information is itself a source of primary reinforcement and call an end to further debate. That would be premature. There is evidence that organisms are even more choosy about the exact type of information on offer. Fantino and Logan (1979) sum up this evidence by suggesting that 'good news' is reinforcing but that 'bad news' is not. This certainly seems to be the conclusion one would draw from those operant experiments which have used so-called 'observing response' techniques. While a pigeon pecks a key for food reward, it may also be able to make another response — pressing a pedal for example — which allows it to observe what schedule it is on. Generally such procedures show that organisms will respond in order to produce stimuli associated with reward, but will not seek out information about stimuli associated with absence of reward. Moreover such lawfulness has relativity built in. Thus if an organism is responding on two schedules, one of which produces less reward than the other, observing will not normally be maintained for stimuli associated with the lesser reward condition.

We have so far considered only those experiments involving positive events such as food delivery. We may well ask whether our conclusions generalize to negative events. The answer would appear, partially at least, to be yes. It is to that area we now turn.

The safety signal hypothesis

In a review of data and theory relating to predictable and unpredictable shock conditions, Badia *et al.* (1979) reach several firm conclusions. Most important is that organisms generally share a preference for predictable over unpredictable shock, even if they cannot do anything to avoid or escape the shock. Moreover the preference is so strong that often animals will choose to endure predictable shocks of far greater intensity or frequency than unpredictable ones. This of course blatantly contradicts the rub-off magnetism theory of secondary reinforcement, which would predict that signals associated with shock should become secondarily aversive themselves. However, at first sight it seems also to contradict our latest conclusions since surely news about shock is bad news?

An apparent contradiction only. Normally a signal which denotes a period of shock-risk will, by its absence, denote a period of safety. Thus in the normal scheme of things the 'danger' and 'safety' signalling aspects of a signal are confounded. However, they can be unconfounded and were so by Badia *et al.* (1979). In one experiment, a signal was made a necessary but not a sufficient condition of shock. In another experiment a signal was made a sufficient but not a necessary condition of shock. What this means is that in the former case absence of the signal guaranteed safety even though its presence did not necessarily entail shock. In the latter case a signal always entailed shock but its absence did not guarantee safety. The findings were that preference for the signalled condition was solely a function of how dependably safety was signalled. Thus in the first condition the signal could be a false alarm 80 per cent of the time and yet this unreliable predictor of shock was still preferred, since its absence was a totally reliable safety signal. By contrast, in the second condition, preference decreased as probability of unsignalled shock increased,

73

thus degrading safety information. We can thus conclude again that it is 'good news' rather than 'bad news' which is reinforcing. Why?

OPTIMIZING STRATEGIES

The world of behavioural science has, at the very least, exhibited a certain amount of excitement during the last decade which we can conveniently date from E.O. Wilson's influential publication: *Sociobiology: the new synthesis* (1975). It does seem, however, extraordinary that one of the core aspects of sociobiology — the tenet that behaviour as well as physical structure is subject to the pressures of natural selection — had remained so undeveloped in all those previous post-Darwinian years. Sociobiology strictly speaking is the application of evolutionary principles to the social behaviour of animals, including man (Barash 1981), but in a wider sense it has encouraged psychologists of all kinds to see behaviour generally in an evolutionary framework: in other words, how might this or that behaviour have had survival value?

From our immediate point of view, a sociobiological perspective enables us to relate by a unifying theme behavioural data from the operant laboratory and more naturalistic field studies undertaken by ethologists. Many animals in the wild will have two major concerns. On the one hand they will need to locate and consume food. On the other hand they will need to avoid falling victim to predators. Both field studies and laboratory studies suggest that animals are very good micro-economists in the way that they allocate the valuable commodity of time spent in goal relevant activities. In the operant laboratory, for example, the use of concurrent schedules has shown us that given the choice between two alternative sources of reinforcement with different pay-offs, pigeons will behave in predictable ways, consistent with mathematical optimizing models. Depending on the exact schedules involved, in some cases the pigeons will uncannily match proportion of time spent on each key to proportional pay-off; in other cases where 'matching' is not optimal, they will maximize the total pay-off by sticking to one particular key.

In the field, researchers have also studied the way in which foraging animals divide up their time between different clumps of food. Once again mathematical models of optimal foraging are given support. In terms of ultimate motivational questions concerning explanations of shifts in behaviour — from one Skinner-box key to another or one clump to another — the notion that evolutionary fitness underpins mathematical lawfulness is an attractive one.

The same arguments that we have seen used to illuminate the question of time allocation between different sources of food can also be used to address the issue of preference for signals. Such preference should be shown in just those cases where signals enable the organism to allocate its time more efficiently between different activities than it otherwise would. Consider that this is exactly what the safety signal hypothesis predicts. Assuming that periods of safety are longer than periods of danger then valuable time can be devoted during the safety period to doing things other than looking out for an aversive event. In the wild, an animal can forage rather than continue to look nervously around. Pursuing this over-simple but illustrative analogy, an animal well informed about safety will both eat well and survive. Organisms also like reward schedules as well as schedules of aversive happenings to be predictable. Once again it can be argued that this is also because time can be allocated more efficiently between food-relevant and food-irrelevant activities.

BEING AN INFORMED HUMAN

As is often the case when psychology moves from animals to man, elegant theories fly out the window. The literature becomes messy, not least because researchers have studied so many different types of information, about mere electric shock in a laboratory experiment on the one hand and about major illness on the other. A list of events, important to humans, which could be made more or less predictable would be endless. And yet whether humans do seek predictability does depend both on the situation and the person. Messiness however does not imply a total absence of knowledge so let us review what is known.

By far the greatest amount of research has addressed the question of whether people prefer to have information and warning about potentially aversive or stressful procedures. This reflects psychologists' traditional interest in the darker side of life. What we do know from a number of studies is that even in identical situations some people prefer information while others do not (Evans *et al*. 1984; Katz and Wykes 1985; Miller 1979a; Averill *et al*. 1977). It may be useful to look for unifying themes in these various studies. One obvious variable which affects preference is controllability. If a person believes that something they can do will help to avoid or otherwise mitigate an aversive event they will be more likely to prefer advance information. This is not too surprising and can be explained with a simpler theory than safety signalling: in essence a warning signal enables a preparatory response to be made. Could it be that even when the situation is objectively the same, different individuals perceive controllability differently and thus show different preferences? Thus some may prefer warning even when it seems on the face of it that nothing can be done about the situation. By contrast, others may prefer not to know about something even if they could apparently do something about it. Thus although controllability-seeking in the widest sense may indeed determine predictability-seeking, it is nevertheless the case that people, unlike animals, have many subtle psychological mechanisms for defending themselves against aversive events. Controllability therefore takes on a richer meaning.

One can control the stressfulness of a potentially aversive event, a surgical operation for example, by busying oneself with thoughts of everything but the operation. Thus distracting oneself may be a means of control for one person while another may seek to control the potential stressfulness of the operation by seeking detailed information about every aspect of it, thereby presumably limiting needless worries and enabling further strategies to be developed for coping with genuine concerns.

We are saying then that information-seeking behaviour in human beings should be seen as part of a wider area of investigation into coping behaviour. Coping strategies themselves often fall into two opposing categories: vigilant or non-avoidant on the one hand and non-vigilant or avoidant on the other hand. Two questions arise. Which type of strategy is most preferred and which type of strategy best reduces stress? The answers, in a nutshell, depend on person and situation.

It would appear that some people are more likely to be information seekers than others. These vigilant copers do not obviously reveal themselves as different on standard personality tests, although there seems to be an over-representation of so-called Type A individuals (a broad coronary risk profile) among their ranks (Evans and Fearn 1985; Evans and Moran 1987a). Vigilant copers can be identified by a specific questionnaire prior to their revealing themselves in a behavioural context (Miller 1979a).

Situation is as important as person. Non-vigilant distracting types of strategy rely on a person being able to ignore or psychologically distance themselves from 'danger cues'. Paradoxically it is more difficult to distract oneself from predictable dangers than unpredictable ones, because time itself provides danger cues. Assuming we all stub our toes on averge once a week, imagine how awful it would be if we knew such stubbings would in future only happen on Wednesdays at 5 p.m. Perhaps not that awful; but imagine that toe-stubbing be replaced by 'possibility of death', in other words you know that when you finally make your exit it will be at this hour. Now finally imagine that you have already had your three score years and ten. We are now dealing with what only a psychologist could term 'an aversive event of high intensity, high probability, and temporally predictable'. Such parameters, we hypothesize, influence choice between vigilance and distraction.

When we replace threat of death by threat of laboratory electric shock we find our hypothesis supported in the case of volunteer human subjects (Evans *et al*. 1984). In this experiment, subjects could choose between being vigilant for a signal that might herald shock or watching a distracting display of interesting information. The number of subjects who chose to distract was greater when it was believed that the shock was less probable. The number was also greater when subjects had some prior experience of the shock — a condition generally experienced as less intensely aversive. Subjects were also distracted more when the threat itself was not shock but aversive noise, that is, a less intense threat.

We have said before that perceived controllability options should influence the choice between vigilance and non-vigilance in the face of threat. Certainly making the shock more or less avoidable in the choice paradigm of the above experiment does indeed affect choice (Averill *et al*. 1977; Evans *et al*. 1984). In the absence of any possibility of avoidance, fewer people want to know when the shock is likely to occur and correspondingly more people choose a distraction strategy.

In everyday terms this tends to make sense. People do distract themselves from even horribly intense threats such as nuclear war so long as they believe them beyond their personal control (or even perhaps convince themselves that such events are unlikely). People also manage to distract themselves fairly well from highly probable aversive events whose intensity however would lead one to call them nuisances rather than disasters: the toe-stubbing and car-starting problems of life. It is interesting to observe that such happenings might be lessened by greater vigilance, but at what cost? A question we address below.

If we have identified the parameters of vigilance behaviour correctly then two issues emerge. First it is possible that situational parameters may provide a clue in understanding the person factor. Controllability, probability, and intensity of threat are ultimately subjectively perceived commodities, and it may be a different perception of them that underlies individual differences in vigilance choice, when the situation is the same for all subjects. We noted that vigilant copers may be more likely to exhibit the coronary Type A profile. It is interesting that at least one major theory of Type A (Glass 1977) identifies in the behaviour pattern an over-developed need to control events; thus Type As will be more likely to perceive control as possible and less willing to recognize helplessness, other things being equal. The second issue or challenge that emerges is to look for a unifying theory which fits the facts. It will already be apparent that the elegant safety signal theory will not do so, at least in an unmodified form. We will approach this goal through consideration of our second question which concerns coping strategy and stress reduction.

COPING AND STRESS

Danger and stress are natural bedfellows. In an ideal world the latter is experienced so long as the former is left unresolved. We could at this point spend a good deal of time trying to pin down the concept of stress by trying on definitions like off-the-peg suits. We might as well try to attire the Minotaur at Marks and Spencer. Instead we will leave it as a layman's term in the belief that this will not compromise the understanding of empirical studies.

Fear, anxiety, stress, and pain, it has been pointed out on many an occasion, are evolutionarily adaptive: they are warning signs and calls for action. They are also of course unpleasant experiences. Moreover in the context of man in a modern society even their positive adaptive role is often no longer apparent. What however needs emphasis here is the original tight linkage between stress reduction and danger reduction. Given that organisms face a complexity of dangers, a good principle to programme into any organism would be one of damage limitation: minimize the maximum damage. Into this equation we would also enter the damages of stress itself. Thus a greater stress in the longer term may be avoided by a smaller stress in the short term. In essence this is the minimax theory put forward by Miller (1979b). It does seem to provide a plausible umbrella under which a number of empirical studies can be viewed. This we now do.

We begin with an item from the *Los Angeles Times*, quoted by Thompson (1981). The city council, aware of how many people seem mildly phobic about travelling in lifts, decided to put notices in its lifts telling people not to worry since there was little danger of them dropping uncontrollably or running out of air. The notices had to be removed a year later when it became clear that they were increasing rather than decreasing stress reactions. In this case the notices gave no details of what one could do in such an eventuality; they only served to remind people of a possible but very improbable eventuality which all but the most phobic would not otherwise think about. The lessons of this real-life experiment have generally been confirmed by research psychologists.

Thus information which serves only to highlight a dangerous or painful state of affairs without increasing controllability will probably serve only to increase stressful arousal. This was certainly found to be the case for cardiac patients who were given lots of information about their illness but no other psychological intervention (Cromwell *et al.* 1977). In a study of forty women about to undergo a stressful diagnostic procedure to check for cervical cancer, Miller and Mangan (1983) obtained similar results. Most strikingly the simple manipulation of highly informing one group and not another prior to the procedure resulted in quite large differences in self-reported distress even five days after the cervical test. The informed group were more distressed. The only possible beneficial effects of detailed information about the procedure were during the medical examination itself, when somewhat less hand-clenching was observed amongst the highly informed group of patients. In this one respect, there is agreement with previous findings concerning the effects of information on the impact of medical examinations (Johnson and Leventhal 1974) and electric shock given to volunteer subjects (Katz and Wykes 1985). Information such as knowing when and where a pain will occur in a definite short-term context can thus be beneficial but lots of information in a more nebulous longer-term context may be counter-productive. Why?

One of the flexibilities of the minimax theory, as Thompson (1981) points out, is that it predicts that under some circumstances control is not preferred. The *Zeitgeist* which reached its apotheosis in the publication of Martin Seligman's book *Helplessness* in the mid 1970s proclaimed that controllability was 'a good thing' for all organisms, lack of control a psychological disaster and a stepping stone to clinical depression. That *Zeitgeist* needs qualification. According to a minimax view controllability is in the service of minimizing stress and danger. If this can be achieved by surrendering control to the expert doctor, the airline pilot, or Fred the trouble-shooter, then the patient, the passenger, and the managing director can stop worrying and still be in superordinate control of the situation by judicious delegation of responsibility. In that sort of context it hardly makes sense to expose oneself to information that can only cause stressful arousal. Thus in certain circumstances, notably when personal controllability is impossible or severely limited, an avoidant coping strategy should be both preferred and less stressful. One qualifying point may be mentioned here, however. Miller and Mangan did find that person variables and situation variables showed some interaction, such that those who were naturally predisposed to monitor for information showed more stress when not informed, whereas the converse was the case for those whom Miller termed blunters — those disposed to avoidant coping.

Such coping is certainly less arousing in the sense of physiological responding by the sympathetic division of the autonomic nervous system. Under threat of possible but by no means certain electric shock, student volunteers who choose a distracting strategy show less electrodermal activity (Miller 1979a) and less cardiovascular activity (Evans et al. 1984), than did subjects who chose to remain vigilant for warning of shock. It is germane to draw parallels here with the work of Paul Obrist and colleagues on cardiovascular reactivity and its relationship to what they have called 'active' coping.

In a typical experiment (for example, in Light and Obrist 1983) subjects are presented with reaction-time tests of differing difficulty in which strong incentives (earning money, avoiding shock) are also present. Results tend to show that cardiovascular arousal is greatest when task difficulty is intermediate. Easy tasks which require little coping evoke minimal physiological response, but so also do tasks which are perceived as almost impossibly difficult and therefore presumably impossible to cope with. Active coping and heightened cardiovascular response are both maximized when some controllability is present but also when uncertainty of outcome exists. This cardiovascular reactivity is also certainly reflective of general sympathetic involvement since the physiological effects are abolished in subjects who have been given beta-adrenergic blocking drugs.

Another researcher in the field of psychophysiology and coping is Marianne Frankenhaeuser. By measuring levels of body catecholamines (adrenalin and noradrenalin) Frankenhaeuser (1980) has in a number of different studies confirmed the correlation of active coping and heightened sympathetic activity. Moreover she coins a useful phrase to describe the process: 'raising the body's thermostat'. Such a phrase steers a convenient course between those awkward words arousal and stress, which no doubt several colleagues would judge a veritable Scylla and Charybdis. To recapitulate, heightened sympathetic activity is linked to forms of coping which involve active strategies such as being vigilant, enquiring, meeting challenges head-on, etc. Much active coping however is routine everyday life. Such ordinary activity as doing a bit of mental arithmetic can be shown to produce an increase in sympathetically mediated heart rate. Frankenhaeuser indeed presents evidence that among groups of schoolchildren sympathetic responsivity is positively correlated with good achievement and adjustment indices. Carroll *et al.* (1984) also present evidence of consistent individual differences among student subjects in heart rate reactivity across tasks where sympathetic mediation is almost certainly involved, for instance playing space invaders. We are obviously not in such cases talking about physiological signs of stress, even though the body's thermostat has, as it were, been raised. But can the body's thermostat be raised for too long and too often, and is this what we mean by stress?

Interestingly, Type A people rear their over-busy heads again at this point. Many have suggested that the link between Type A and the ultimate physical pathology, which is coronary heart disease, lies in Type A persons showing chronically elevated levels of sympathetic activity (Matthews 1982). Excessive levels of catecholamines constantly circulating in the bloodstream may aggravate the arterial damage which is a precursor of coronary heart disease. Frankenhaeuser certainly reports that while normal subjects and Type A subjects both respond to active coping tasks with the expected pattern of sympathetic activity, nevertheless Type A subjects take longer to 'unwind' — they maintain higher levels of physiological activity even when it is no longer appropriate. Slow unwinding has also been shown to characterize cardiovascular activity among Type A subjects (Evans and Moran 1987b). It is also interesting that in more everyday coping at work, a pattern of slow unwinding characterizes poor copers. Such findings come close to what the layman commonly believes about the relationship between stress and illness. Are there similar findings regarding other physical pathologies?

Ulcers in particular are often seen by the lay public as caused by stress. However, the research here tells a complex story. Brady (1958) reported what has become a seminal and celebrated study of so-called executive monkeys. The climate of opinion in the 1950s was that business executives were good exemplars of a stressful profession. Since stress was taken to be a causative factor in ulcer development, *ipso facto* executive responsibility should be associated with a greater incidence of gastrointestinal ulcers. Brady and his colleagues devised an experiment to test this hypothesis. Monkeys were assigned either to an 'executive' group, in which a monkey was responsible for avoiding an electric shock by pressing a lever, or they were assigned to a 'yoked' control group. The essence of the control group was that for each executive monkey there would be a control monkey who would avoid the shock when the executive made 'correct' decisions and suffer the same shock as the executive when the latter failed to respond correctly. Even those who may with some justification object to the ethics of this kind of animal experimentation will note the elegance of this experimental design. Both groups of animals are exposed to absolutely identical 'physical' stress; the difference between the two groups is solely a 'psychological' one. Brady did indeed find greater evidence of ulcer development in the executive group, suggesting that the monkeys that had to cope 'actively' with the source of stress were at greater risk.

Unfortunately in other respects Brady's experiment was not well designed. Crucially, monkeys were not randomly assigned to each group; rather monkeys who seemed to be good at learning operant responding found themselves in the executive group. Thus it is possible to argue that the executive group started out with more ulcer-prone monkeys in it. Brady's basic yoked design was, with improvements, taken up by another researcher in the 1970s, namely Weiss. However, this decade had a different perspective on things. We have already noted the influence of Seligman's notion of helplessness: organisms seek controllability and the perception of lack of control is stressful. The hypothesis of the 1950s is turned on its head: we now would predict that the non-executive group who passively receive shocks with no control over them will develop more ulcers. Broadly speaking, and using rodents rather than monkeys, this is what Weiss (1977) reports. We seem then to have a certain amount of ambiguity. Were Brady's results totally due to experimental artefact? Perhaps, but the hypothesis of the 1950s does seem to square with the findings thirty years later which link active coping and psychophysiological responsivity. In fact it is Weiss's own work which suggests a resolution. Controllability was not the only variable to be associated with ulcer development in Weiss's series of experiments. Another important variable may be called 'effortfulness' of response. Thus if executive subjects have to perform particularly difficult responses where outcomes are uncertain then Brady's pattern of results is more likely to emerge. What emerges then when we survey the totality of evidence presented in this chapter so far?

SUMMARIES

First we can identify across species a desire for predictability and controllability. These commodities are often but not always stress reducing, subjectively and physiologically. Sometimes, however, active coping styles which seek to exert control may be counter-productive in terms of the subjective stress they engender and certainly in terms of possible long-term effects of heightened physiological arousal which accompanies such coping. Counter-productiveness is increasingly to be expected when active coping has to be or has become chronic, and where the coping is effortful and/or uncertain in its efficacy.

Alternatives to active vigilant coping have not so far received much attention except in the form of distraction. However, we have also said that distraction under some conditions is difficult — when, for example, a threatening event is highly aversive, highly predictable, and highly likely. We may well ask what we can do about coping with a threatening situation which we cannot put 'out of mind'.

This indeed is a fitting topic with which to conclude our chapter since it addresses a literature which takes us into a more purely cognitive domain, where the subjects of experimentation are perforce human. The area was pioneered in the 1960s by Richard Lazarus and involves the crucial concept of 'cognitive appraisal'. Between stimulus and response to threat, there is the meaning which a human being attaches to that stimulus. Even very extreme life-threatening events are not immune to the mediating power of appraisal. The Christian martyr may 'see' a different fire from the wretched putative witch.

Lazarus' experiments (see Lazarus 1974) were on a more modest scale. Subjects were shown films of distressing material, notably an aboriginal circumcision ritual, or an industrial accident in a carpentry shop. The films were accompanied by different sound-tracks for different subjects, so as to encourage different appraisal processes. In some cases the sound-track emphasized the aversiveness of the events depicted, and in these cases physiological responses were greater than when no sound-track at all was presented. Other sound-tracks however sought to deny the aversiveness of the events, or alternatively delivered the details in a detached and technical way. Such sound-tracks, which were meant to encourage denial or intellec-tualization, were found to reduce physiological arousal compared to no sound-track. Thus cognitive appraisal mediates physiological reactivity. Subjects who had the chance to rehearse the events in imagination before the films were also more adept at lowering physiological response. Indeed one of the major behavioural methods of treating phobic reactions — systematic desensitization — relies on exposing oneself to the imagined situation in a controlled way prior to *in vivo* practice: some of this treatment's success may well depend on coping skills being acquired through a re-appraisal process as well as the learning of relaxation skills (Goldfried and Davison 1976). Equally a much quoted report by Janis (1958) suggests that while denial styles of coping can reduce stressful reactions by hospital patients in the short term prior to surgery, in the longer term they may be counter-productive in not encouraging the more realistic appraisal that reduces stressful reactions after surgery. In all these cases appraisal is however an important mediating concept affecting stressful reactions, be they short or long term.

It should come therefore as no surprise that the relationship between real life stressful events and physical and mental health is not a perfect one, since one person can appraise an apparently stressful event differently from another, and even positive events can have a stressful component in so far as they may be disruptive of valued routines. Notwithstanding such a caveat, much research has stemmed from Holmes and Rahe's (1967) notion of a social readjustment scale on which a person's recent accumulation of significant life events can acquire a numerical value to be compared with others. A crude relationship does exist between such measures and indices of health. However, interpretation of work with these easy-to-use rating scales is fraught: sometimes it is not clear whether, say, a depressive illness episode should be seen as following from an event or events, or alternatively as perhaps being involved in causing the events — earlier signs of depression may, for example, have contributed to job loss. Using proper structured interviews avoids most of the serious problems. A trained interviewer can better establish exact timings for events, and can also report on how an individual appraises those events.

It suffices to say that such messy but more real-life research backs up the laboratory work on coping and stress. Much more accurate predictions of stressful effects of life events can be obtained when subjective appraisal is taken into account by using interview assessments, rather than bald counts from a pre-published check list.

CONCLUSION

With cognitive appraisal processes we have moved far from the operant laboratory where we began this chapter. The aim has been to provide an integration of a number of different research 'literatures' which too often are treated separately from each other. Loud objections that people are not laboratory rats have become customary of late. Indeed it is the species call of a certain kind of fiercely anthropocentric first-year student. However, readers may, it is hoped, have been a little persuaded that when it comes to mastering and making sense of their environment they should not necessarily feel themselves in a totally different universe from more humble members of the animal kingdom.

8

An energizing force?

Most of us have no difficulty in accepting, at least as a useful metaphor, the notion of acutely felt biological needs such as hunger 'driving' us to activities designed to meet that need. Indeed the experiential aspects of compulsion, of being driven, are well attested by those who have felt and reported on episodes of food deprivation. The shipwrecked sailor alone on the Pacific, air-crash survivors marooned in the remote Andes, volunteer 'neolithic' subjects isolated in an anthropological field experiment — all have described the way in which hunger came to dominate every perception, every action. The sailor caught and ate the most unappetizing raw fish as if it were the greatest delicacy; the air-crash survivors overcame the strongest taboos concerning cannibalism and ate the air-crash victims; the volunteer subjects finally broke the rules governing their experiment and sought to poach a sheep from the neighbouring farmland. *In extremis* then we can talk meaningfully of a force acting on us: the parallel with the language of physics is germane.

In its quite proper concern to develop as a scientific discipline, psychology, and particularly the psychology of motivation, has sought to widen the notion of 'driven' behaviour to include all behaviour, not just *in extremis* varieties. Put succinctly, driven behaviour is determined behaviour and science has traditionally been deterministic.

No founding father of modern psychology was more influenced by this concern than Sigmund Freud. Reared in the Helmholtzian world of late nineteenth-century medicine which believed that all forces acting on the organism could ultimately be reduced to physical-chemical ones, Freud sought to produce a psychology of motivation which was both deterministic and biologically based. Together with his colleague Josef Breuer he put forward an early theory of motivation which saw all behaviour as seeking to preserve a constant and optimal level of central nervous system activity. Deviations above or below this optimal point of tonic activity produced agitation and effort to return to the optimal point. In this early theory Freud strikingly foreshadowed theoretical developments in academic psychology which were not to come to the forefront until after the Second World War.

There were others who also and contemporaneously put forward theories which suggested that stimulation gives rise to different levels of sensation and affect which can be more or less optimal in terms of felt pleasure (hedonic tone) and efficient learning and performance of tasks. Wundt (1893) on the basis of experiments in which subjects reported their sensations to different intensities of stimuli (for example, temperature, pressure, taste, smell), concluded that hedonic tone was related to stimulus intensity by an inverted U function, whereby increases in intensity would be seen as increasingly pleasant up to a certain optimal point, but further increases in intensity would be perceived as increasingly unpleasant. The implication for an hedonic theory of motivation — and most theories have been hedonic — is that people will seek to optimize pleasure. Two psychologists, Yerkes and Dodson (1908), explored the further implication that efficiency of learning and performance would be maximized at some optimal point when stimulation is sufficiently intense to engage the necessary processing mechanisms, but not so aversively intense as to disrupt such processing. They showed in addition that the exact pattern of the inverted U function depended on the difficulty of the task. Their results, using mice as subjects, indicated that electric shocks of differing intensity interacted with the difficulty of a visual discrimination task in determining the number of errors made. Thus in a simple task, learning continued to be better with increasing levels of shock up to a point well beyond that which was optimal for a more difficult task. We shall postpone further discussion of optimal 'arousal' theories till later in this chapter, since, for reasons that might exercise the skills of an historian, they appeared only largely to disappear again for many decades. Meanwhile Sigmund Freud changed tack, and later gained a strange bedfellow in Clark Hull, whose theory of motivation dominated many experimental psychology laboratories in the 1930s, and indeed beyond.

Freud continued to propose a theory of motivation based squarely on a hedonic, a pleasure, principle, but his ideas of what constituted pleasure changed. Perhaps for reasons connected to an ingrained pessimism, perhaps through an easy parallel with obvious drives such as hunger and thirst, Freud came to see pleasure as deriving from a

87

diminution of stimulation. Thus the sexual impulses which Freud saw as being at the core of virtually all motivation were pleasurable only in so far as they were satisfied, that is, reduced. The whole of the psychic apparatus was geared up to reducing libidinal tension consciously and unconsciously, in obvious ways or disguised ways, successfully or unsuccessfully. Tracing the vicissitudes of the sex *Trieb* (better translated as drive rather than instinct) through the free associations of neurotic patients became the art but not perhaps the science of psychoanalysis. At this juncture it is relevant only to concentrate on the motivational core of Freud's theory which sees stimulation reduction as the ultimate aim.

By stripping Freud's early theory to its essentials in this way we can more easily see how he came to his final and deeply pessimistic theory of motivation. Amid the carnage of the First World War, he began to think differently about aggressive and destructive behaviour. In his earlier theory such behaviour resulted from the thwarting of the all-pervading pleasure principle. He now suspected that destructive impulses were more deeply ingrained in humankind, and were not just mere vicissitudes of libidinal struggles. He posited the existence of two drives: Eros — the life-seeking, and Thanatos — the death-seeking. The former obeys the pleasure principle and in its positive aspects pleasurable quiescence follows engagement in the living world. The death drive Freud saw as a deep regressive pull on the organism to return to the inorganic state; it followed a 'nirvana' principle, seeking the very ultimate in peaceful undisturbed quiescence. Freud saw destructive behaviour as a desperate attempt on the part of an individual to fight the pull of Thanatos by projecting destructive impulses outwardly against others. Speculative and unrefined, Freud's later ideas were not in the main accepted by his followers. (A notable exception was Melanie Klein, who did embrace the concept of the death instinct.) For us, the closing words on Freud's life and death instincts can come from Zuckerman (1979): '[they] might be regarded as a metaphor for the common observation that the activity of organisms can be seen as either an attempt to increase or reduce stimulation and internal excitement.' With that we are back, but too soon, to optimal theories.

Clark Hull was not an optimal theorist. Like the middle-period Freud, he believed in a single drive force, which goaded an organism — most often a white laboratory rat — into activity. Like Freud, he believed that the ultimate aim of such activity was to reduce the internal stimulation which was hypothesized to represent the drive. Learning or conditioning occurred in so far as behaviour which successfully reduced drive was thereby reinforced; it developed habit strength and would be repeated in similar future circumstances. Unlike Freud, Hull did not identify drive with any particular source, let alone a sexual source. Instead any state of bodily need could serve as a source of drive. Thus if an animal's need to avoid danger were aroused — perhaps by a warning stimulus associated in the laboratory with electric shock — at the same time as it was hungry, Hull would see both fear and hunger as sources which would pool together to produce a measured amount of non-specific drive energy. The notion of a non-specific energizing force is given a good deal of support by experiments which show, for example, that a mild amount of fear can increase the vigour of eating (Gray and Smith 1969), that hunger can facilitate responding designed to avoid shock (Meryman 1952), that thirsty animals continue longer than controls to make a bar pressing response, which has been learned under conditions of food deprivation (Kendler 1945).

Hull's theory starts getting into trouble when it asserts that all goal-directed activity seeks to reduce drive levels. What about rats which learn to press bars for saccharine, which has no nutritive drive-reducing properties? And what, more fundamentally, of a whole range of behaviours which can be considered under the rubric of curiosity? If the world of animals is sufficient to embarrass Hullian theory, the world of man is enough to devastate it, so many are the examples from roller-coasters to horror movies of sources for increases of stimulation. That is not to say the drive theorists did not fight back. First of all they could point to the role of associative conditioning in producing secondary drives and secondary reinforcers. The difficulties of this line of approach are discussed elsewhere in this text. More deviously some spoke of a need for curiosity giving rise to drive, in the same way as need for food does. But such theorizing becomes tortuous if one still wishes to keep the notion of drive reduction allied to some reduction of internal source of stimulation. Increases of stimulation paradoxically become sought after in order to reduce stimulation. At the behavioural level it seems sensible to keep the truth simple: organisms often seek high levels of stimulation for its own sake and not *en route* to an hypothetical drive reduction. At the neurophysiological level, meanwhile, discoveries were being made which would transform Hull's drive concept and generate new theories about how behaviour may be energized.

THE CONCEPT OF AROUSAL

The demise of Hullian drive theory in academic psychology took place at the same time as growth of motivational theories centred on the concept of arousal. We have already seen how early in the century Yerkes and Dodson had hypothesized a central motivational state of the organism which related to the efficiency of performance at a variety of tasks. This concept of arousal was taken up by many theorists in the 1950s and 1960s, but what was common to all of them was a desire to link behaviour and physiology. The discovery by Moruzzi and Magoun (1949) of the 'arousing' function of the reticular formation area was a spring-board for the development of a number of arousal theories (Hebb 1955; Duffy 1957; Lindsley 1957).

It will be remembered from our discussion of sleep research that Moruzzi and Magoun showed that stimulation of the reticular formation would wake a dormant animal. Further research showed that this so-called ascending reticular 'activating' system (ARAS) received direct input from the senses: for example, a visual stimulus translated into neural form is routed in the normal way to the visual cortex, but also goes direct to the ARAS. Hebb's theory thus described two functions of sensory events: a 'cue' function which specifically guides behaviour, but also a general 'arousal' function. Sensory stimulation then serves to activate or alert the organism in a general way, independent of the exact nature of the stimulus. On this view, stimuli act via the ARAS to charge the cortex, thereby encouraging vigilance and alertness.

However, arousal theorists took up the notion of Yerkes and Dodson that arousal could be too high as well as too low. They thus posited descending influences from the cortex to the reticular formation which would regulate the stimulation of the cortex by external and internal sources. The reticular formation could then be seen as a kind of arousal homeostat (Lindsley 1961). Optimal arousal theory, therefore, was reborn with a neurophysiological underpinning. Cortical arousal, as indexed for example by electroencephalographic records, is seen to be governed by reticular control mechanisms.

Few concepts in psychology have proven so bothersome and yet so superficially attractive. On the positive side it would appear that we have a psychological concept which makes sense of an array of data, suggesting that both performance and felt pleasure are optimized at certain moderate levels of arousal. Moreover we appear to have means, through the EEG for example, to measure arousal independently from its assumed effects on performance and preference.

Negatively the concept has been constantly undermined by its all-embracing character, as both a physiological and psychological construct. Measures of behavioural or self-reported alertness do not always correlate well with cortical measures of arousal. There are even disagreements amongst psychophysiologists about which EEG measures might best constitute a measure of arousal (Gale 1981). When we consider peripheral physiological activity, such as heart rate and skin conductance, there is even more ambiguity, for not only do these measures often fail to agree with central nervous system and behavioural measures of arousal, they often do not correlate well among themselves (Lacey 1967). This does not mean to say that the concept of arousal is a dead one in modern psychology, far from it; but it does mean that the use of the term has necessarily become qualified over the years. At the very least one speaks of behavioural arousal, autonomic arousal, and cortical arousal, knowing that even within these 'systems', measures of arousal are often decoupled from one another — let alone across systems. It is against this background of terminological complexity and empirical openness that we must proceed. We turn first to the relationship between arousal and performance.

AROUSAL AND PERFORMANCE

The growth of arousal theory took place at the same time as a wealth of experimentation into human factors in job performance. The demand during the Second World War for quick and accurate answers to problems meant that those same problems were brought straight into the laboratory for analysis. Psychologists were asked to investigate factors influencing the vigilance of radar operators, the efficiency of production workers, etc. This applied aspect of experimental psychology was thus set to grow steadily in the post-war years.

One particular area of research which is relevant to arousal theory concerns the effect of what might be called 'stressors' on performance. What is the effect of stressors such as noise and sleep deprivation on task performance? Let us first of all consider the findings themselves and then see whether the notion of arousal is a helpful one in pulling the findings together into a plausible theory.

Broadbent (1971) presents a detailed review of the experimental evidence. As may be expected, both noise and sleeplessness can have a deleterious effect on the performance of a number of tasks. What is much more interesting is how the two factors interact with each other. Wilkinson (1963) had subjects perform a serial reaction-time task under different combinations of noise and sleep deprivation levels. In a serial reaction-time task, the subject must make the correct response to one of a number of stimuli; when the subject makes a response this automatically leads to another stimulus being presented. The results of the experiment showed that errors increased over a half hour period if subjects were deprived of sleep or if the conditions were noisy. However, if subjects were sleep deprived and exposed to the noisy conditions performance was better than if only sleep deprivation had taken place. Thus noise helped to reduce errors when subjects were sleep deprived, but increased errors when subjects had slept normally.

In vigilance experiments (for example, Broadbent and Gregory 1965; Corcoran 1963) noise and sleep deprivation have again both been shown to lead to a deterioration of performance but have also been shown to exert their effect in different situations. Thus noise tends to hinder performance when many signals are presented during the vigilance period, whereas sleeplessness hinders performance when the signals are few and far between.

What do we make of such results? It is tempting to assume that both sleeplessness and noise are affecting a single mechanism which controls the arousal of the organism. If optimal arousal theory is correct then arousal can be too low or too high. Sleeplessness can be assumed to be associated with low arousal, whereas noise is seen as increasing the level of arousal. Thus a sleep-deprived subject may benefit from additional noise by virtue of arousal being increased from a sub-optimal point; by contrast noise may hinder performance under normal circumstances by increasing arousal beyond an optimal point. There are other converging lines of evidence which add plausibility to this use of arousal as a unifying hypothetical construct. Broadbent (1971) mentions in particular results from experiments where subjects perform tasks under high incentive conditions which would be expected to increase arousal. There is evidence that very competitive tasks where subjects' motivation to succeed is keenly engaged can have deleterious consequences, consistent with the notion that arousal is supra-optimal (see also chapter 9). Equally there is evidence that sleep deprivation effects are minimized in high incentive conditions, whereas noise effects are maximized. Thus another factor: incentive, which is also plausibly linked to a common-sense concept of arousal, appears to interact with sleep deprivation and noise in just the way predicted by optimal arousal theory.

It is tempting to 'physiologize' at this point, despite our previous caveats, and suggest that, notwithstanding other complexities, all three factors affect some reticular-cortical mechanism. Poor performance due to too low arousal is readily explained on this view: the cortex needs a constant flow of messages from the reticular formation in order to maintain alert wakefulness; noise increases such stimulation; sleepiness decreases it. Even embarrassing findings hinted at earlier that peripheral physiological arousal may be out of tune with inferred behavioural or cortical arousal can perhaps be accommodated with a little ingenuity. There is evidence that sleep deprivation is often accompanied by heightened arousal as measured by peripheral physiological measures, notably skin conductance (see Zuckerman 1979). However, it may also be hypothesized that such resulting internal sensory feedback may be used by a central arousal mechanism in the same way as it uses external stimuli, that is, to increase arousal from a low point. But there are good reasons not to overdo any too easy marriage of behavioural and neurophysiological findings. First, we have already remarked on the difficulty of consensus on what might constitute a proper measure of cortical arousal. Second, neurophysiology does not so easily tell us how over-arousal disrupts performance. Third, we shall see that as we broaden the scope of arousal theory, the idea of a tonic (or background) level of arousal responding to adjustment by a single mechanism and related to performance by an inverted U function is too simple to accommodate all the evidence. Let us then broaden the scope.

THE ROLE OF INDIVIDUAL DIFFERENCES

One of the major figures in personality research in the post-war era has been Hans Eysenck. Eysenck's theory of personality has been closely linked with the concept of arousal, in particular his dimension of extraversion. Eysenck bases his fundamental personality dimensions, including extraversion, on innate differences in nervous system functioning. Initially he was strongly influenced by theoretical aspects of Pavlov's work, and also the behaviour theory of Clark Hull. He identified the genotypic differences between introverts and extraverts as lying in the balance of cortical excitation and inhibition, with introverts being balanced more towards excitation and extraverts towards inhibition. Pavlov had noted many years previously individual differences in the conditionability of dogs. Some seemed friendly, co-operative and interested in everything, whereas others seemed more reserved and timid. To his surprise Pavlov found that the former type were less good during conditioning trials; they took longer to acquire conditioned responses, which were then more easily extinguished. The more reserved dogs, by contrast, proved to be eminently conditionable. Pavlov explained these differences in terms of cortical excitation/inhibition balance. If excitation dominates then the dog (or in Eysenck's theory: the introvert) will respond to stimuli at lower thresholds; in a sense the nervous system can be seen as 'weak' and easily bombarded by stimuli but also responsive. If inhibition dominates (as supposed in the case of extraverts), then stronger stimuli are needed to reach an activating threshold; the nervous system can be seen as 'strong' but sluggish. This idea of types of nervous system became established in Soviet psychology and as we see was reflected in Eysenck's original theory. Eysenck (1967) went on to update his theory in line with neurophysiological developments and now saw the differences between extraverts and introverts as differences in cortical arousal mediated by the reticular formation. To simplify somewhat, extraverts were seen as chronically under-aroused and needed extra stimulation to perform at their best; introverts were seen as chronically over-aroused. At this point we need not concern ourselves with the many other aspects of Eysenck's theory such as the relationships among extraversion, hedonic preference, and arousal. We stay with the relationship between arousal and performance.

There is a good deal of evidence which confirms Eysenck's theory. For example Revelle *et al.* (1976) found that introverts outperformed extraverts on an intelligence test when a placebo (inactive) 'drug' was given to subjects. When, however, a genuine stimulant drug (caffeine) was administered extraverts were superior to introverts. It is plausible to suggest that under the placebo condition the extraverts were sub-optimally aroused and therefore performed worse. With caffeine, however, the extraverts are pushed nearer their optimal point, while introverts are pushed beyond it and hence the order of merit is reversed.

Another major individual difference variable, long recognized by psychologists, concerns 'anxiety'. Clearly we all feel anxious at times when we perform different types of task, an examination being an obvious example of a task which is often accompanied by high levels of anxiety. In addition however there appear to be reliable and stable differences between individuals in their anxiety-proneness. We can distinguish then between something called 'state' anxiety — the anxiety a person feels at a certain time — and 'trait' anxiety — an enduring personality factor disposing towards anxiety in general. In Eysenck's theory this personality factor is labelled 'neuroticism' and in his earlier writings is identified with the arousability of the autonomic nervous system. How then does anxiety relate to efficiency of performance?

If we hold for the moment to some central arousal mechanism we may suppose that anxiety heightens arousal and thus will be related to performance by the good old inverted U function. In layman's terms we may expect that moderate levels of anxiety can give the edge to performance but that high levels can be disruptive. There is indeed some evidence not only for this simple view but also for the more developed notion given by the Yerkes-Dodson law outlined earlier. Spence and Spence (1966) studied the joint effects of anxiety and task difficulty on performance of paired-associate learning. In such tasks the subject must learn to respond to a stimulus word with a specific response word (for instance: table-chair). Task difficulty was manipulated by having word-pairs which were naturally associated as in the example just given, or ones where no natural association was present. The researchers found that high anxiety was associated with superior performance of an easy task, but inferior performance of a difficult one. This is of course consistent with the idea that the optimal point of arousal for an easy task will lie higher on the arousal dimension for an easy task than a difficult one. Spence and Spence had originally planned their experiments within the framework of Hullian drive theory and interpreted their effects in terms of high drive blindly energizing all responses. In the case of the difficult task it is possible to see this as being defined by incorrect responses competing with correct ones: high anxiety/drive thus serves only to energize wrong responses bringing them nearer to threshold. Although such a Hullian formulation is now outdated, it does, as we shall see, have echoes in more recent theories of attentional control in relation to arousal.

The layman may not be too surprised by these findings. They suggest for example that a little anxiety may help motivate certain well-rehearsed behaviour. The actress who has learned her lines well, the student who has revised his notes diligently, may both have an edge given to their performance when the real thing takes over from dress-rehearsal or mock examination. Contrarily, anxiety may be a disruptive influence when preparation has been less adequate.

PROBLEMS OF AROUSAL THEORY

We have discussed a number of variables which we have supposed to influence an inferred state of arousal. The list has not been exhaustive but the reader may perhaps be impressed by the apparent usefulness of the arousal concept. Instead of having to talk separately about the effects of x, y, and z on performance, it seems we can more parsimoniously talk about performance being influenced directly by one central motivational state.

Theoretical parsimony must always be sought in any scientific discipline and indeed the clarion call for parsimony was given way back in the fourteenth century by that wily Franciscan friar and philosopher William of Occam: 'Pluralitas non est ponenda sine necessitate.' (Plurality should not be posited unless necessary.) The question which modern psychologists have to answer is whether all the existing data can be handled by a theory so simple as arousal theory.

Our dilemma is well put by M.W. Eysenck (1984): 'We are left in a rather frustrating situation: there is sufficient behavioural equivalence across arousers to support an arousal based theory, but the overlap is not great enough to justify any simple arousal theory.'

Frustration however is not the same thing as pessimism. The psychologist is frustrated because he knows too much, not too little. At the simple pragmatic level, a psychologist wishing to apply his problem-solving skills may get a good deal of mileage out of simple arousal theory. He or she can make educated guesses about the effects of stressors and personality on performance, being guided by the nature of the task under investigation. Even if the arousal concept refuses to be pinned down to some clear physiological reality, at the very least it offers a kind of notebook rubric under which the psychologist can marshal and organize a variety of diverse findings. Seen as a 'first approximation' theory it may even offer a valuable structure for better appreciation of what does not fit the theory. Let us now turn in that direction.

Simple arousal theory seems to be strongly supported by those studies mentioned earlier where two stressors are looked at in interaction. Thus noise improves performance in sleepless (assumed under-aroused) subjects, but hinders performance in normal subjects. Incentive, likewise, can counter the effects of sleeplessness. There are however oddities which have been noticed in regard to such findings. Many researchers for example have commented on the efficiency with which sleep-deprived subjects perform a variety of tasks. Incentive, far from merely countering supposed effects of sleep deprivation, often abolishes effects. Another oddity is that, in a typical vigilance situation where a subject is constantly monitoring for the appearance of a signal, both noise and sleep deprivation are alike in not having any effect until well into the vigilance period. If a single background state of arousal were a major determinant of performance it is hard to explain why two opposing stressors both fail to have an effect immediately.

Such anomalies have led Broadbent (1971) and others since to posit at least one extra arousal system. Broadbent conceives of two arousal mechanisms: upper and lower level. The lower level mechanism is affected by noise and sleeplessness in the way we have already envisaged. However, the effects of the lower level mechanism can be compensated for by the upper mechanism. The lower level executes well-established decision processes, whereas the upper level mechanism monitors and adjusts the lower level. Thus observed performance does not directly relate to the immediate state of the lower simple arousal mechanism, since the stressors which are assumed to be affecting it are at the same time being compensated for by the upper mechanism. Broadbent would then see any deterioration as a gradual process which only appears as the upper mechanism itself suffers inefficiency by its prolonged efforts to compensate. Together with further speculations concerning the role of other arousal related variables, this two storey model has been echoed in other recent theorizing. For example, Humphreys *et al.* (1980) distinguish two 'activation' states: a general arousal state but in addition a more focused state reflecting what they term 'on-task effort'.

When we turn to the effects of extraversion on performance, we begin to realize why even those who are wedded to arousal theory are all agreed on the need to move beyond a simple version of it. A fairly robust interaction has been found between extraversion and time of day in terms of their effects on performance. It is known that efficiency of performance relates to diurnal rhythms, in particular that of body temperature. Performance is usually worse in the morning when body temperature is low and improves as the day progresses and as temperature rises. That this diurnal variation relates to some arousal state is given support by the fact that introverts usually outperform extraverts during morning testings, while extraverts do better than introverts later in the day. This suggests, as a preliminary hypothesis, that introverts, with their assumed higher arousal level, can compensate for the otherwise low (sub-optimal) arousal conditions of morning testing sessions. Later in the day, however, introverts find themselves over-aroused compared with extraverts.

However, this interpretation that extraversion and time of day are both independent inputs affecting the same arousal mechanism is not one that can be sustained. If we accept that body temperature reflects the state of arousal, it seems that extraverts and introverts do not on average differ with respect to arousal, but rather show a different pattern of change, with introverts reaching their peak earlier than extraverts. The performance data also supports a more complex relationship, if we consider additional interactions. If, for example, we try to increase arousal by testing subjects in a group or administering a stimulant such as caffeine, we find predictable results during morning testings: extraverts improve their performance relative to introverts. We would expect however that introverts would do especially worse if afternoon testing and another arouser (group testing or caffeine) were combined. This is not however the case. Figure 5 illustrates

Figure 5 Verbal ability mean scores as a function of personality, drug condition, and time of day

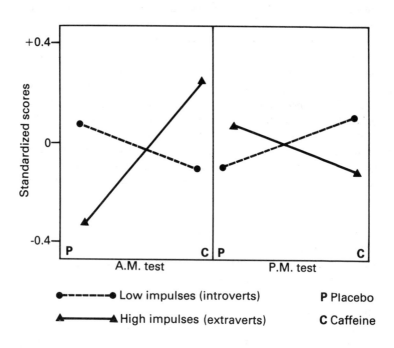

(After Revelle *et al.* 1980)

the results of an experiment by Revelle *et al.* (1980). The results for morning testing on their own are understandable on a simple view: the superiority of introverts is reversed by caffeine. The results for subjects without caffeine are also understandable: introverts do better in the morning, extraverts in the afternoon. What is totally at variance with a simple theory is the result for caffeine and afternoon testing: introverts outperform extraverts.

If we wish to keep the construct of arousal in the light of such complexity we must at the very least agree with Broadbent (1971) that extraversion is a condition which will affect arousal *under certain conditions*. Such a view is also reflected in Eysenck's more recent writings, where he sees the main difference between extraverts and introverts not in terms of chronic arousal levels but in arousal *potential*. The difficulty with regard to arousal theory is to make exact predictions. Eysenck (1981) has made some attempt to do this by hypothesizing a non-linear relationship between arousal potential and actual arousal. Such a view predicts that extraverts will have lower levels of arousal than introverts when the environment is itself a low-arousal one, but that extraverts will have higher levels of arousal than introverts in high-arousal environments.

Arousal potential theory has indeed met with some success in its predictions (see Smith 1983) but still has difficulty explaining interactive effects on complex cognitive tasks (see, for example, Matthews 1985). One of the problems with assessing any inverted U function, such as the Yerkes-Dodson law or the hypothetical relationship between arousal potential and arousal, is that of over-fitting. By suitable *post hoc* assumptions many findings can be interpreted as supportive of the theory. Another critical point which we touched on earlier with regard to arousal theory concerns our asking how arousal has its effects on performance. In particular how does high arousal disrupt performance? In asking such questions we are naturally led into a new level of analysis and investigation. As we have said already, arousal theory provides a useful but over-simplified rubric for bringing together diverse findings; it even permits rough and ready predictions to be made. However, ultimately, by the word 'performance' we usually mean the end product of a number of processes: receiving sensory information, processing it, retrieving information from memory, making decisions on the basis of information, and finally executing a response. Finer predictions about the effect of so-called arousers can only come by addressing these dimensions of performance.

Thus it seems that a whole array of so-called arousers do indeed have a common effect on that element of performance which could be called 'attentional selectivity'. Attention becomes more sharply focused on certain aspects of a task to the exclusion of others when noise, high incentive, or anxiety attend the execution of a task. By contrast selectivity is reduced in sleep-deprived or extravert subjects. This pattern however is not consistent for other aspects of performance. Sleep deprivation reduces speed of performance, a characteristic shared this time with introversion rather than extraversion. Most arousers which do increase speed (noise, incentive, performing later in the day) show what is called the speed/accuracy trade-off: gains in speed are accompanied by a sacrifice in accuracy. However, sleep deprivation which is associated with reduced speed is not necessarily associated with greater accuracy. Anxiety is also anomalous: less accuracy for no gain in speed — this is perhaps due to increased distractibility or lack of attentional control in anxious subjects. Anxiety and sleeplessness also result in impaired ability to hold items in temporary memory store and also impair more long-term memory storage. Anxiety in particular also impairs the efficiency with which material can be retrieved from memory. By contrast, 'arousal' due to noise or time of day impairs short-term storage but improves long-term storage and retrieval efficiency. This rather complex picture is schematically presented in Table 3.

What then are our conclusions? We now know that different arousers do have differing effects on different cognitive processes. We also know from the evidence already discussed that different arousers often combine together to produce complex interactions, rather than simply adding their effects to each other; in other words one arouser is not like a teaspoonful of honey added to another of white sugar and another of brown sugar to produce an extra sweet mixture. It remains to be seen therefore, and is indeed a matter of current debate as to whether the future lies with theories stressing different arousal systems, or in the abandonment of arousal concepts altogether. The suspicion remains that for some time at least psychologists will operate their explanatory vehicle with two classes of ticket. Quite often there is loose agreement between central nervous system, autonomic nervous system, and behavioural indices of heightened arousal. Quite often performance is predictably related to arousal. If we ignore the 'memory' portion of Table 3, we can perceive a good deal of consistency in the effects of diverse arousers. Such a second class ticket can thus provide us with some decent mileage. However, arousal (and, indeed, an arousal system) is in the end an explanatory concept, not a thing. It follows therefore that the

Table 3 Effects of 'arousers' on performance

	TYPE OF 'AROUSER'					
	Time of day	White noise	Incentive	Introversion	Anxiety	No sleep loss
Type of performance						
PERCEPTUAL-MOTOR						
Increased attentional selectivity	?	yes	yes	yes	yes	yes
Decreased attentional control	?	?	yes	yes	yes	?
Increased speed	yes	yes	yes	no	zero	yes
Reduced accuracy	yes	yes	yes	no	yes	zero
MEMORY PROCESSES						
Short-term storage improvement	no	no	yes	zero	no	yes
Long-term storage improvement	yes	yes	zero	yes	no	yes
Retrieval more efficient	yes	yes	zero	no	no	?

'No sleep loss' is so categorized to draw attention to consistency of attentional affects across 'arousers'; the reader should thus infer that sleep deprivation (traditionally a 'de-arouser') will have opposite effects. 'Zero' indicates no effects. '?' indicates uncertain effects (After M.W. Eysenck 1984)

theories in which they are embedded do not become wrong when we move to more complex findings; rather such theories become inadequate.

AROUSAL-SEEKING BEHAVIOUR

We now return to the idea that arousal is also related to a hedonic dimension, as well as to performance. Here too in the 1950s it became a central notion that people sometimes acted to increase arousal and sometimes to decrease it. This as we have noted is in contradiction to earlier 'drive' theories of Hull and Freud. The impetus for a change in theoretical views undoubtedly came most from a desire to explain that large class of behaviours which can be called 'curiosity': exploration, approaching novel and complex situations, activities such as play, and so on.

A number of psychologists put forward related and overlapping theories to account for such behaviour. Some (for example Hebb 1955) emphasize the background (tonic) state of arousal as important. Thus if this is too low, stimulation will be sought so as to increase it to some higher level, whereas if the background level is too high, efforts will be made to reduce it. Other theorists, notably Berlyne (1960, 1967), based their theories on the pleasurable or aversive quality of short-term changes in arousal. Such theories stress the importance of arousal potential. Thus 'boredom' (for Hebb a 'too low' arousal state) is for Berlyne a non-optimal state which generates high aversive arousal. This, in his early theory, is like Hullian drive: stimulation is sought to reduce it. Berlyne thus explained such behaviour as riding roller-coasters as seeking so-called arousal 'jags'. High arousal is sought just so that it can be reduced — the pleasure of mastering fear as it were. Berlyne was finally forced to admit, however, that in many cases we see that increases in arousal can be pleasurable even though arousal reduction does not immediately follow. Berlyne's later theory moved decisively in a direction which has continued in more recent theorizing: away from the hedonic qualities of change in some presumed cortical arousal towards an underpinning in those areas of the brain most clearly linked to pleasure and pain, namely the limbic system.

Berlyne supposed that novel and potentially arousing situations automatically had the capacity to stimulate neurons in both the 'pleasure' and 'pain' systems of the limbic brain. If we suppose however that the pain system has a higher threshold for activation then something equivalent to an inverted U function can be inferred by summating activity in the two opposing systems. This is illustrated in Figure 6. While the pain system is still below threshold, pleasure continues to increase with arousal potential, but as soon as the pain system comes into action it begins to bring the net amount of pleasure down from its optimum. Finally the pleasure system is outdone by the pain system and further increases in arousal potential will be clearly felt as aversive.

A major element of Berlyne's theory and other short-term (phasic) change theories is that both increases and decreases of stimulation

Figure 6 Supposed effects of novelty on pleasure and pain systems

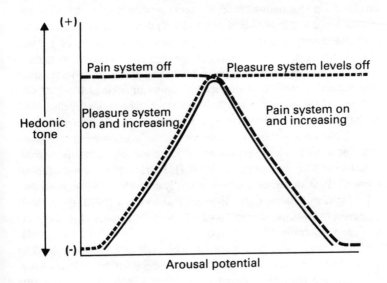

Solid line shows resultant hedonic tone from summation of pleasure and pain systems.

from the background level are seen as potentially pleasurable; thus sudden changes associated, for example, with the recreational use of a depressant drug may be sought out as much as the effects of a stimulant drug. Further illumination of this kind of theory can best come from considering two further research questions. First, can arousal-based theories shed light on what most people would agree are clear individual differences in the degree to which people seek out thrills, excitement, and novelty? Second, since we all, including the greyest man in the street, occasionally feel like taking something akin to a roller-coaster ride, is there any theory which illuminates such motivational changes within the individual? This is the question of intra-individual differences. We address each question in turn.

INDIVIDUAL DIFFERENCES IN AROUSAL SEEKING

We have already discussed the role that extraversion has played in relation to theories of arousal and performance; it is not therefore surprising that this same personality dimension has been seen as involved in mediating arousal seeking behaviour. It will be remembered that in H.J. Eysenck's (1967) theory arousal was linked at the neurophysiological level to cortical activity mediated by the reticular formation. Extraverts could be seen as biased towards under-arousal and therefore would be motivated by and large to increasing stimulation in order to bring arousal up to an optimal level. If we assume that this implies a level of arousal *felt* to be optimally pleasant, we have a prediction that extraverts will be more likely than introverts to seek out arousing situations involving thrill, excitement, novelty, etc. There does indeed seem to be evidence for this supposition from a variety of sources (see Eysenck 1967). Extraverts are, for example, more likely at an earlier age to be sexually explorative, to begin smoking — in fact in the words of Eysenck and Eysenck (1975) the typical extravert 'craves excitement, takes chances, often sticks his neck out . . . and generally likes change'.

Views about the neurophysiological bases of extraversion however, particularly as they relate to hedonic aspects of behaviour, have followed the path seen already in Berlyne's later theory: towards limbic system structures. Foremost among contemporary theorists is Jeffrey Gray. Gray (1971) has suggested that the limbic area of the brain is crucially involved in the regulation of approach and avoidance behaviour through distinct 'stop' and 'go' systems, linked to punishment and reward. In Gray's view extraversion represents a relative weakness in the strength of the 'stop' system. Put crudely: extraverts are strong on pleasure but weak on fear. Note that this is a relative statement and does not refer to the absolute strengths of the motivational systems. Eysenck's second major dimension of personality, 'neuroticism', does refer to absolute tendency to react emotionally. Indeed neuroticism is sometimes termed 'emotionality'. Gray's view is pictorially presented in Figure 7. Note that the dimension of anxiety in Gray's schema is the diagonal dimension whose high-end pole comprises persons who are predisposed to react more emotionally than average (high neutoricism) and in whom fear of punishment is likely to outbalance hope of reward (low extraversion).

Gray's theory extends Eysenck's initial one along lines which seem intuitively attractive when talking about such matters as exploration and curiosity. It does seem that novel or ambiguous or risky situations will evoke competing motives to approach and avoid. That extraversion differences exist in such behaviours suggests that the neurophysiological basis for extraversion should indeed lie in the

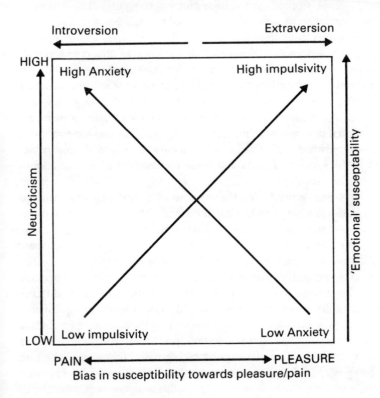

Figure 7 Gray's diagonal dimension of anxiety expressed in terms of neuroticism and extraversion, and their assumed theoretical bases. Also shown is 'impulsivity' expressed as the opposite diagonal

balance of those systems outlined by Gray.

Another researcher who has made a particular study of individual differences in this area is Marvin Zuckerman. Using standardized questionnaires he has sought to identify individual differences in what he terms a 'sensation-seeking' motive. In his more recent theorizing concerning the biological bases of sensation-seeking (Zuckerman 1979), he has also largely abandoned an optimal cortical arousal theory and moved his speculations along lines which draw closely on Gray and other contemporary neurophysiological psychologists: 'down the pathway of biological hedonism', as he puts it.

Zuckerman's sensation-seeking scales (SSS) however should not be identified too closely with Eysenck's extraversion scale. They do of course correlate with each other but only weakly (median r = 0.29 from a number of studies cited by Zuckerman 1979). It seems that SSS measure something more akin to what amounts to a component of Eysenck's broad extraversion dimension, namely 'impulsivity', a predisposition to acting on the spur of the moment and taking risks — a picture consistent with an underlying nervous system tuned to expect reward rather than punishment. However, things are muddier when we consider the relationship between emotionality and SSS. Referring back to Gray's schema in Figure 7 we see impulsivity as another diagonal dimension, with its high-end pole in the high extraversion-high neuroticism corner. A simple equation between this diagonal dimension of impulsivity and sensation-seeking might suggest a positive, albeit weak, relation between SSS and neuroticism. Yet Zuckerman predicts and finds no evidence of any relation to sensation-seeking. Why?

It seems sensible for the purpose of elucidating the nature of sensation-seeking to distinguish different aspects of neuroticism as well as extraversion. Neuroticism is often taken as a broad measure of trait anxiety as well as emotionality. Anxiety, as we shall see in a moment, cannot be left out of the picture.

If we bring theory down to earth for a moment we should remember that Zuckerman's scales do successfully predict a variety of different behaviours which the layman would very sensibly group together under some term such as sensation-seeking: volunteering for unusual experiments, parachuting, diving, preferring complex drawings, listening to loud music, experimenting with illicit drugs, smoking, being interested in erotic films, gambling, etc. Many of these activities are risky, therefore can we simply say that sensation-seekers are below the norm on anxiety and therefore are less scared of taking risks?

The evidence as we have said points to no relationship between SSS and neuroticism. Moreover if we treat the scale as an emotionality scale and if we equate high impulsivity with jointly high emotionality and extraversion then even less do we expect a negative relationship between neuroticism and SSS, since SSS is clearly linked to impulsivity. With respect to anxiety, perhaps we need to be more specific.

Zuckerman in fact shows that sensation-seeking scores are correlated negatively with those kinds of anxiety scales which ask about specific fears relating to concrete and often physical threats to safety. Sensation-seeking is not however related to the kinds of social fears most often tapped by general anxiety inventories. Thus it remains possible that the sensation-seeker is indeed an impulsive: high on extraversion and high on a specific aspect of emotionality which excludes reference to fears of impersonal dangers and threats.

Even so, Zuckerman's concept of sensation-seeking is in the end not the concept of arousal-seeking with which we began, and the individual differences in SSS are not to be simply identified either with Eysenck's extraversion scale or with Gray's diagonal impulsivity dimension. Sensation-seeking, for example, seems also to be related to Eysenck's newer personality dimension of 'psychoticism' (tough-mindedness). Males score more highly on both psychoticism and SSS, and both Eysenck and Zuckerman have speculated on the role of male sex hormones in the biological bases of their dimensions. At its extreme psychoticism is allied to cruelty, impersonal detachedness, and other elements of what clinicians term 'psychopathy'. It is possible perhaps to see Zuckerman's extreme sensation-seeker as a person with a very low boredom threshold, who therefore impulsively seeks out thrills, is relatively fearless when faced by impersonal dangers, and who possibly avoids interpersonal anxieties by only relating superficially to his fellow human beings.

INTRA-INDIVIDUAL DIFFERENCES

Notwithstanding personality-type 'biases' in who does and does not tend to seek higher degrees of arousal, it is also the case that we all find ourselves at different times in moods where we seek out arousal in the form of stimulating company, an exciting book or film, a sports activity, or something else. In our work environments, we may on some days see problems as challenging and approach them with an enjoyment akin to playing a game. At other times our mood is very different. We see problems as potential sources of stress, which we approach seriously and with a view to ending them and the arousal they engender as quickly as we possibly can. We return to our homes possibly with the intention of lowering the remnants of such aversive arousal even further. We seek enjoyment in relaxing to music, immersing ourselves in a hot bath, or simply putting our feet up and closing our eyes. In short depending on our mood, we can all of us sometimes be arousal seekers, sometimes arousal reducers. What do psychological theories say about this inconsistency within individuals?

Clearly optimal arousal theory may itself be invoked as offering some sort of explanation. What we have hazily called mood may correspond to our current position on an arousal dimension. If our position is below optimal, we are under-aroused and seek to increase our level to get nearer the optimal point. If we are above the optimal point we seek to lower it. A simple optimal arousal theory of this kind however fails a rather basic test for a theory which claims to be a psychological one: it does not square with the experiences which seem to go with the behaviours under consideration. When people seek thrills and excitement, these states in any common-sense formulation correspond to rather high levels of arousal, not to some neutral middle point of an inverted U function. Similarly when we seek to relax we are seeking what is surely a rather low level of arousal. Although theorists such as Berlyne coined terms such as 'arousal jags' to try to reconcile high arousal seeking, there seem to be serious problems for an optimal 'sought' arousal theory which seeks to keep any kind of ordinary meaning attached to the word arousal.

There are other experiential anomalies. Optimal arousal theory, put in this simplistic way, suggests that certain key feeling states, such as boredom, relaxation, excitement, and anxiety, all lie on the same arousal dimension. If they do, and if we agree that the first and last of these are aversive, while the middle two are positive, then we end up with a theoretical inverted U of the kind illustrated in Figure 8. Thus boredom is a state of arousal which is lower than relaxation and so low that it is felt as aversive. Similarly excitement is a state of arousal not so intense as anxiety. Do such theoretical predictions square with reality of experience? Surely we speak sometimes of nagging anxiety, not a description which implies the heights of arousal? Even more odd is the implication, for example, that as acute anxiety subsides it passes through a stage of excitement.

These kinds of difficulty were exactly those which led M.J. Apter to put forward a comparatively recent alternative to optimal arousal theory (Apter 1982). In essence optimal arousal theory, as we have just outlined it, is a simple homeostatic theory. The optimal point is the setting of the homeostat at some non-extreme middling point. We seek therefore a stability based on being motivated to seek or reduce arousal as fluctuations take us out of the optimal range. Apter suggests that we recognize the experiential anomalies, abandon a simple homeostatic view, but retain the language of cybernetics (the language of control systems).

Apter suggests that we invoke the principle of 'bistability': 'A system exhibits bistability if it tends to maintain a specified variable, despite external disturbance, within one or another of *two* ranges of values of the variable concerned. This contrasts with homeostasis in which only *one* range of values is involved' (Apter 1982).

Figure 8 Mood state positions according to simple inverted U hypotheses

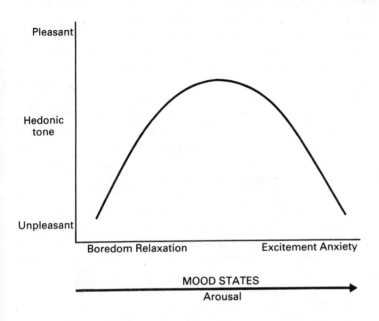

Apter goes on to posit two systems (at root biological, though this is speculative) which determine which range of values is being maintained. These systems underpin two metamotivational states: telic and paratelic. The phrase metamotivational state implies something not itself motivational but which determines a pattern for motivated behaviour. In the telic state (from the Greek word *telos* meaning goal) the individual is said to be orientated to reaching goals, activity is seen as merely a means to an end, and the mood is serious-minded: in such a state arousal is something ultimately to be reduced. In terms of Figure 8, the individual is motivated to get to the low arousal 'relaxation' point of the arousal dimension. In the opposing state (called paratelic) the individual is said to be orientated towards activity for its own sake, and the mood is playful; in such a state high arousal is seen as positive and to be sought out. In terms of Figure 8 the individual is motivated to get to the high arousal 'excitement' point of the arousal dimension. They are seen as occupying similar positions,

109

which are however experienced differently according to metamotivational state. The theory is represented diagrammatically in Figure 9.

Figure 9 Hypothesized relationship between arousal and hedonic tone, depending on meta-motivational state

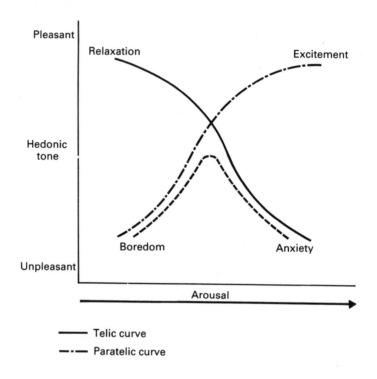

(After Apter 1982)

One of the strengths of Apter's theory is that it avoids some of the pitfalls of arousal theory by keeping the meaning of the arousal dimension fundamentally tied to the experiential domain. It is in essence a theory about 'felt' arousal. That does not of course exclude biological speculation. Another of its strengths is seen in its concept of so-called reversals.

Reversals take place when the telic state suddenly changes to paratelic or vice versa. As a result, the quality of felt arousal changes: relaxation may change to boredom, excitement to anxiety. In this way Apter's theory has echoes of Schachter's theory of emotion (see chapter 6). Hedonic tone is something akin to a labelling of arousal consistent with the current state, telic or paratelic.

Apter provides examples of the sorts of situations in which reversal theory seems to provide a useful explanatory framework. A man enjoying a high state of sexual arousal during intercourse (paratelic 'mode' operative) may suddenly see his performance as some kind of test, whereupon there is a shift to telic 'mode' and high arousal is experienced as anxiety, which will in turn disrupt further enjoyable sexual activity. A mountaineer may be enjoying high arousal — excitement — until he notices a danger which he may not be able to control; excitement turns to anxiety and the goal of getting off the rock face becomes uppermost.

Apter's theory provides a promising framework for looking at what has often been neglected in psychology: the inconsistency of much behaviour at the individual level. It has already generated a good deal of experimental research and measures of metamotivational state have been developed. At the very least those of us who are interested in predicting behavioural and psychophysiological response to 'arousing' situations such as threats, promises, challenges, etc. — a big area of experimentation — might do well to think in terms of Apter's central telic/paratelic distinction. Its consideration during the course of an experiment may help to organize that 'noise' in our results which often comes from the different meanings imposed on the experiment by different subjects. Whether the subject is serious-minded or playful at the time may be a useful guide to predicting many kinds of responding.

A final point should be made. Apter at first glance seems to move into the same field as Eysenck and Zuckerman when he points out that, despite his two modes, it is probably correct to see individuals as biased towards one mode or other. Murgatroyd et al. (1978) developed a scale to measure such bias called the 'telic dominance scale'. We might expect this scale to correlate (inversely of course) with extraversion. After all, the extravert is supposedly an arousal seeker, and the telic dominant individual an arousal avoider. Unfortunately for those who like simplicity, there appears to be no relationship between these two measures. As with extraversion and sensation-seeking, it seems that we are dealing with different measures. The only common ground, and the reason why all three individual difference measures come together in this chapter, is that they all have roots in the arousal concept. The telic dominance measure however is ultimately a reflection of the biases an individual perceives in the way he or she experiences the world; whereas extraversion and sensation-seeking scales are more concerned with predicting behaviour.

CONCLUSION

The conclusion that telic dominance is not merely extraversion by another name provides a useful springboard for ending this chapter. It reminds us of the theme that has run throughout the review of theory and research into both performance efficiency and hedonic preference. The theme is simply that there is no single agreed thing called arousal. Different theorists may spell out with greater or lesser precision the nature of hypothetical arousal systems which are parsimoniously designed to explain a limited range of findings. For the rest, and for the purposes of this chapter, the word arousal remains an ordinary English language word which can still however serve as a useful rubric for bringing diverse findings together.

9

Achieving, succeeding, failing, and persisting

In this chapter we address areas of research in psychology which many would see as most germane to any book on motivation: striving for success and achievement. A quick reflection should easily convince the reader of how wide and pervasive a topic this is. Human beings spend a great deal of their lives pursuing very conscious goals, and, on the whole, feel very good when these are achieved and not so good when failure is encountered.

Goals can be short term or long term; they can involve the workplace and career advancement; they can involve family and domestic matters; they can refer to a leisure or sporting activity. In the case of all goals, however, we can divide the factors that determine success or failure into two classes: those which we would see as motivational and those which we would not. Take academic achievement, for example. It is obvious that people have a better chance of such achievement in our society if they come from a higher socio-economic class, if they have enjoyed better schooling, and, assuming that all are not born equal, if they have greater native ability. These and other factors make up the class of non-motivational determinants of achievement. However we all know that even when individuals appear to be matched fairly well on these sorts of factors, even when we can assume some realistic equality of opportunity, there are nevertheless those who seem to achieve more simply because they try harder, persist longer.

Predicting these key motivational phenomena, persistence and effort, has been the theoretical challenge prompting much empirical work by psychologists over forty years or more. Some of the work has been done within quite distinct theoretical traditions: for example that involving an apparently measurable motivational construct which has been called 'need for achievement' (nAch for short). More recently researchers have looked to a study of 'cognitions' to explain individual differences in persistence and effort. Other researchers have distinguished between extrinsic motivation (doing things for external rewards such as money) and intrinsic motivation (doing things for their own sake). Such motivational distinctions have led in the same direction towards the predicting of effort and persistence behaviour.

In this chapter we shall review the evidence from these different traditions of enquiry. The founding tradition is that which rests on the concept of a general need to achieve, and it is this tradition we look at first.

A NEED FOR ACHIEVEMENT

Maslow (1954) was responsible for classifying human needs in a hierarchical fashion. At the bottom of the hierarchy are survival needs (for example, for food, water, air). Next come security needs, followed by needs for love, affection, and affiliation. Then come competence and mastery needs, and finally self-actualization needs. The major assumption of Maslow's scheme is that higher needs become the focus of interest to the degree that lower level needs have already been satisfied, a point we come back to later in this chapter. Achievement-related needs occupy the competence and mastery rung of Maslow's ladder.

How then can we go about measuring the strength of someone's need to achieve (hereafter shortened to nAch)? Historically the tendency to see human behaviour as the outward expression of inner psychological needs and tensions was very much associated with psychodynamic theory. For this reason, the first attempts to measure nAch made use of a projective test, devised by a psychodynamic personality theorist called Murray. The test is called the 'thematic apperception test' (TAT). The idea behind the test is that subjects tell a story about each of a series of pictures presented to them. The assumption of psychodynamic theory is that since the pictures themselves are deliberately ambiguous with respect to meaning, the themes that make up a person's stories will have been 'projected' from the person's own psyche and will therefore reflect their most important current needs and concerns. Thus the person who is currently very much concerned with achieving, succeeding, etc., should put more achievement themes into his TAT stories. The question is: Does the TAT as a measure of nAch have reliability and validity?

McClelland et al. (1953) in their classic book on the achievement motive certainly consider that counting up achievement themes in the

TAT is a reasonably reliable measuring instrument. The key reliability index is whether two judges independently 'scoring' sets of stories can come up with the same totals for subjects. The answer would appear to be yes, provided guide-lines in the form of a manual are followed. Consistency of scoring across different TAT pictures is more problematic, as is test-retest reliability (the extent to which nAch scores given on one occasion to a group of individuals are comparable with scores obtained ι n a later occasion). However, as long as a reasonable number of pictures are used it can be argued that weak internal consistency can be lived with. Regarding test-retest reliability, one does not necessarily expect a dynamic motivational trait, such as nAch, to be as stable as perhaps some personality traits, its level will fluctuate according to particular circumstances. The question of reliability of TAT and other would-be quicker measures of nAch is discussed in detail by Fineman (1977). It is certainly true that many of the original nAch researchers still consider the TAT to be the most reliable instrument for tapping reasonably stable individual differences in the strength of nAch.

The question of validity — whether nAch measures really do predict achievement-related behaviour — is of course the core of our concern. A host of experiments in the 1950s and 1960s established nAch as a useful predictive construct, especially when simple group comparisons were made between high and low nAch scorers. Thus high scorers solved more anagrams (Lowell 1952), and high-scoring children were more likely to delay an immediate reward in order to achieve a superior reward later on (Mischel 1961). Two experiments in particular, however, came to have a significance for later developments in achievement theory.

First French and Thomas (1958) showed that high nAch subjects would persist longer at trying to solve what (unbeknownst to them) were impossible anagrams. The importance of this experiment was its choice of dependent variable: persistence was taken up by later cognitive theorists as the key to understanding individual differences in task motivation. Persistence has obvious implications for long-term achievements but in the short term can be defined as the outcome of continuous decisions taken by the subject as a result of immediate failure feedback. Cognitive motivation theorists were going to be very interested in how people evaluated success and failure feedback.

The second experiment was one of many performed by one of the key researchers and theoreticians in the area of achievement motivation: J.W. Atkinson. Subjects were tested for recall of tasks performed in the laboratory on an earlier occasion. Of particular concern was recall of tasks which the subjects had not been able to complete. There is an effect in psychology known as the Zeigarnik effect: that people's memory for things left uncompleted is better than their memory for things completed. Atkinson reasoned that, to some extent, the Zeigarnik effect probably reflects concerns to 'do things properly' and 'finish off what one has begun' and therefore might be expected to be particularly pronounced in high nAch subjects. The interesting finding that Atkinson reports is that this prediction is only borne out when the instructions introducing the task performances deliberately strove to engage the subjects' nAch. In fact when instructions were given which deliberately attempted to relax the subjects into an easy-going attitude to the tasks, it turned out that later recall was better among the low nAch subjects. Atkinson reasoned therefore that nAch engaging instructions might be doing more than simply motivating the high nAch people, they might actually be inhibiting the perform-ance of low nAch people. Atkinson's theory was prompted to take into account not just a motive to achieve success by approaching challenges, but also a motive to avoid failure by avoiding challenges. This latter motive was termed fear of failure.

Both nAch and fear of failure (measured usually by questionnaire) are seen in Atkinson's theory as reasonably stable motivational traits. They give us therefore a general rough and ready prediction about how a person might behave in any situation involving challenge, and potential success or failure. However, people have very different levels of general ability and also have differing specific abilities. However high my own nAch may be, for example, I might consider myself incapable of easily acquiring the considerable skills involved in smoothly plastering a wall. A highly successful theoretical physicist may be reduced to the most incapable of bystanders as the AA mechanic handles the breakdown. The point is that our nAch is not engaged equally by every challenge that life throws up. Atkinson therefore suggests that the actual strength of a tendency to approach a situation with a view to succeeding depends not only on our need to achieve (the value that we place on success) but also on the cooler more dispassionate assessment of our likelihood of succeeding (the expectation of success). For this reason Atkinson's approach, still a very influential one, is known as expectancy-value theory.

In fact the theory is strikingly reminiscent of Clark Hull's motiva-tional theory, but tailored to a more circumscribed area of enquiry. Like Hull's drive concept, born out of biological need, we have here nAch, a driving force born out of psychological need. Like Hull's notion of habit strength, born out of prior experience in the learning situation, we have in Atkinson's theory the person's assessment of their probability of success, often born out of memories of previous similar experiences of challenge. Hull however recognized a third important variable in goal-directed behaviour: incentive. Atkinson likewise suggests the importance of incentive and moreover relates incentive directly to the person's expectation of success.

Consider a very easy task where you are likely to succeed nine times out ot ten. We can represent this in exact terms as probability of success (Ps) = 0.90. How would you feel about succeeding at such a task? You certainly want and expect to succeed, but if it is that easy you are not going to be over-impressed with your success, in other words the kudos (incentive) is actually quite small. Consider now a very difficult task where you expect to succeed only one time in ten (Ps = 0.10). If against the odds you do succeed you probably will feel overjoyed. The incentive this time is large. Thus Ps and incentive (I) are perfectly but inversely related: as one goes up the other goes down. We can therefore very easily assign a numerical value to incentive: we simply make $I = (1 - Ps)$. Thus if Ps = 0.1 then I = 0.9; if Ps = 0.2 then I = 0.8 etc. The question is how to optimize both. How do we keep a realistic chance of succeeding but not make things so easy that we feel no sense of accomplishment? The common-sense answer — that we seek out middling degrees of difficulty — is also the one given by mathematically multiplying Ps and I. The product is greatest when both are 0.5.

We have so far however only considered a person whose dominant motive is nAch. We have however noted that some persons may be more concerned to avoid failure, whose natural tendency is to avoid too much in the way of challenge. What predictions can we make for these persons? They will seek to assess the probability of failing: as this goes up they will naturally have a greater dislike of the situation, other things being equal. But of course other things are not equal. Just as there can be different degrees of kudos attached to succeeding, there can be different degrees of shame (negative incentive) attached to failing. Paradoxically, when a task is known to be very difficult (let us say probability of failure (Pf) = 0.9) there should be less shame attached to failing. There is the get-out clause: failure was likely anyway, but at least I had a go. Contrarily if the task is very easy, failure would leave one extremely shamefaced. Thus as with the success analysis, so also here: Pf is related to negative incentive in a perfect but inverse fashion. So we have the prediction that a person's worst fears are aroused by middlingly difficult challenges, where probability of failure and shame attached to failing are both moderately high. Easy challenges are preferred because failure is unlikely; very difficult challenges are not so bad because shame attached to failure is minimal.

Atkinson's theory makes specific predictions which have received encouraging support from both laboratory experiments and real-life studies. Atkinson and Litwin (1960) got subjects to play a game of skill involving tossing a ring over a peg. Subjects were allowed to choose their own distance from the peg when throwing. The prediction that high nAch subjects would more consistently choose to stand at middling distances from the peg was confirmed. In a study of career aspirations amongst college students, Malone (1960) showed that subjects whose nAch was relatively greater than their fear of failure motivation were rated as far more realistic in their aspirations compared to subjects who were relatively higher on fear of failure motivation. Judgements of realism were made independently by careers counsellors and lack of realism could be shown by the student's aiming too high or too low.

Other real-life studies have also been supportive of Atkinson's theory: thus high nAch students more consistently choose middlingly difficult options in their degree studies, and high nAch pupils prefer streamed school classes (where a child will find things neither too easy nor too difficult as measured against his or her peer group). Thus in vocational studies and the laboratory, it would appear that Atkinson's expectancy-value theory has predictive power. Moreover the theory has been developed over recent years (see Atkinson 1981) to much greater degrees of complexity.

One of the major difficulties faced by the simple version of the theory is that it predicts that persons whose fear of failure is greater than their nAch will avoid all challenges, which is hardly the case. Atkinson acknowledges however in his more recent work that external concrete rewards such as money and possessions exist for achievement and these provide an additional source of 'extrinsic' motivation, which complements the 'intrinsic' motivation concerned with pride in success and shame in failure. We address the issue of extrinsic versus intrinsic motivation a little later in this chapter. Suffice it to say here that it is by no means certain that extrinsic sources of motivation can simply be added to intrinsic ones. There is evidence that in some circumstances at least intrinsic and extrinsic sources of motivation interact detrimentally with each other.

Another point addressed by Atkinson's developed theory concerns what we might call the 'dynamic' aspect of striving behaviour. When we have a sequence of successes or failures, we must constantly be re-assessing the key variables in Atkinson's original 'static' formula. What we thought was easy we now consider more difficult and vice versa. Shall we have another go, or do we throw in our hand? The theory was therefore extended to take such dynamic factors into account. On this issue Atkinson is right to point out that the heart of motivational research is not to predict behaviour as an end in itself, but predict whether someone will carry on with behaviour *x* or move on to behaviour *y*. Atkinson makes the obvious parallel here with the animal research which we have referred to in chapter 7, where it is possible to predict the time allotted to different reinforcer-producing activities by considering how total reinforcement may be maximized.

Much of the experimental work that supports Atkinson's model involves inferences that the subject will perceive probabilities of success and failure in the way that the experimenter expects: this may involve giving explicit norms for performance on some task which it is assumed the subject will believe (even if the experimenter has faked them). In other situations the probability of success is fairly obvious; for example, in the ring tossing game described above everyone knows that it gets easier and easier as the player stands nearer and nearer the peg. However, things are not always so simple. Cognitive psychologists interested in motivation have therefore been concerned to investigate how people process information about success and failure and how this effects their assessment of likely future success and failure. It is to this area of research we now turn our attention.

COGNITIVE-ATTRIBUTION THEORY OF MOTIVATION

Weiner (1972) has been foremost in encouraging this development in motivation theory. Attribution theory is not so much a theory in the normal sense, but more a constructive belief that predicting human behaviour can become a more powerful business by finding out the 'causes' to which people 'attribute' their own and others' behaviours. Much research in social psychology in the 1970s and 1980s has involved looking at such perceptions. The contribution of attribution theory to motivational psychology has centred on people's attributions for the causes of their own successes and failures. If someone fails at a task, and is asked why, he or she may give many different kinds of reason for failure. Weiner (1972), however, suggests that many of the reasons can be seen as belonging on two principal dimensions: locus of control, and stability.

The first dimension, locus of control, stems from the earlier work of Rotter (1966), which suggested that there are some people (internals) who for the most part believe that they and others have a large say in their own destinies, and there are other people (externals) who tend to believe that chance factors and uncontrollable events largely shape personal destiny. Weiner asserts that people use this dimension when assessing individual successes and failures: was it to do with me, or not? Moreover these attributions have significance for affect: we feel good if we attribute success internally and we don't feel too bad if we can blame others or bad luck for our failures. The other way round things are not so nice: we do not like to be responsible for our own failures, and we equally are not so proud when we owe our success to others or to luck. Thus attributions can be ego-enhancing or ego-deflating, depending on our use of this dimension.

Weiner's second dimension, of stability, is important not so much for affect as expectation. Perceived causes of success and failure can be divided into those which are largely fixed and those which are largely variable. If we attribute an event to something fixed then we will have no reason to believe that the outcome will be any different next time; if, however, we attribute an event to something variable, then clearly the outcome may be different next time. It is with regard to failure outcomes that this dimension takes on great importance, for it promises to explain individual differences in that commodity which we mentioned earlier as supremely central to any motivational theory: persistence. Persistence means carrying on despite temporary set-backs. Attribution of failure to variable factors translates itself into the belief that a set-back is indeed only temporary.

Locus of control and stability are seen by Weiner as independent dimensions. Thus attributions can be fixed-internal, fixed-external, variable-internal, variable-external. Figure 10 shows how this 'crossing' of the two dimensions gives rise to four main classes of causative attributions: ability, task difficulty, effort, and luck. The first two are relatively fixed; they are not going to change with regard to a particular task. The last two are variable, and could well change on any future attempt at the task. Ability and effort are clearly internal, brought to the task by the person in question, task difficulty and luck are external and beyond the person's own control.

In order to test whether people are indeed more likely to persist if they attribute failure to variable rather than fixed causes, Weiner *et al.* (1972) induced repeated failures on an experimental task. After

Figure 10 Principal types of attribution for success or failure as a function of internal versus external locus of control, and fixed versus variable (stability) dimensions

	Internal	External
Fixed	**Ability**	**Task difficulty**
Variable	**Effort**	**Luck**

each failure, subjects rated each of the four 'causes' in terms of importance in explaining the immediately preceding failure. They were then asked to estimate their likely expectation of success for the next trial. As failure followed failure it was obvious that expectation of future success went down and down. However, it was found, as predicted, that decline in expectation was greater for those who rated either ability or task difficulty as the more important factors in explaining past failures. This seems to support Weiner's view that it is the stability dimension which determines expectation and thus probable perseverance.

How do the predictions of Atkinson's model translate themselves into attribution theory terms? A person high in nAch may be considered a person who particularly wants to succeed and make internal attributions for success (the affective dimension). This could mean attributing success to ability or effort. In the longer term we may suppose that self-perception as an able person is an important part of self-esteem for a high nAch scorer. However, we must also consider how a person can come to gauge how able he or she is.

Someone who is learning to play chess is unlikely to make proper progress and ability assessment by playing constantly with someone who usually loses, or with a grand master who constantly wins. The novice will therefore — in accordance with Atkinson's model — choose matches where the outcome is nearer 50:50. In attribution theory terms these are situations where the most salient internal determinant of outcome is likely to be effort. The persistence on which successful achievement rests depends on keeping effort to the fore as a causal attribution. Thus nAch as a trait-like variable becomes merely an attributive style and in the immediate term knowledge of a person's causal attributions for recent successes and failures is what enables us most closely to predict future intentions: having another go at a laboratory task, carrying on to A levels, taking up maths, dropping maths, or dropping out of everything. (Of course we are only dealing with intrinsic motivation at this point. Mary might continue with maths because Grandma has promised her a new bicycle if she does.) Within such limitations we are saying that attributions will tell us about Mary's feeling for maths and her expectations about maths. These in turn will help predict whether she enrols for the advanced course.

We are giving these internal cognitive attributions quite an important role to play. Trait motives such as nAch and fear of failure might determine how a person is likely to make attributions, but, when all is said and done, it is the attributions which directly determine the next piece of behaviour. We should therefore now ask the important question, asked by Covington and Omelich (1979): Are causal attributions causal?

If attributions do play a causal role in determining achievement behaviour, and if relevant trait variables, such as nAch, are really only pre-dispositions to attributing in certain ways then we should be able to trace a causal pathway to future achievement behaviour in the face of failure. This is illustrated in Figure 11.

Figure 11 Causal pathway via which nAch is assumed to influence future motivation and performance

nAch → Attributions for → Future → Future
           Past Failure   Expectancies   Performance

So those who are relatively higher on nAch compared with fear of failure should be more likely to attribute failures to temporary setbacks, that is, variable factors. Low effort — not trying hard enough

— is one such attribution which is also of course internal and within one's own control. The locus of control dimension is assumed to mediate affective processes, and in this case 'shame' is seen as the causal effect of not having tried hard enough. Bad luck does not lead to shame but it is also a variable factor like effort. Thus both lead to a feeling that things might be better next time. So much for the model; what about the facts?

The Covington and Omelich findings did not support the theory. Students who had failed a course test and had opted to re-take it were asked to rate the causes of their previous failure in terms of Weiner's attributional elements. They were also asked to rate their degree of shame at having failed the test once, and to give their grade expectation for the re-test. The results showed that expectation of doing well and shame at having failed previously both led to better re-test performance as predicted by the model, but expectancy and affect were not related to attributions in the manner suggested. High nAch students did do better than low, but this had nothing to do with their attributions. They also had higher expectations of doing better, once again this having nothing to do with attributions. Finally the only really significant attributional tendency shown by high nAch subjects was a tendency not to put past failure down to a lack of ability but this did not in itself predict performance. How might we interpret these results? One possibility is that in such public circumstances some subjects are using attributions to defend their ego in the face of failure. The attributions in the short term are not therefore used informatively by the subjects to influence future behaviour. It is interesting that high nAch subjects maintained in their attributions a sense of their own ability and had high expectations of success. It is possible that these variables themselves are shaped informatively in the longer term by attributions for past outcomes in achievement related contexts. In the short term, however, attributions may operate retrospectively, their main purpose being to rationalize the past rather than guide the future. Such a view receives additional support in studies by Eccles (1983) where variables such as perceived self-competence and high expectation are the immediate variables affecting intention to enrol in an advanced course of study, but self-competence might well be shaped by a person's habitual style of attributing causes for successes and failures over a longer developmental period. Thus attributions may start off as important mediators of motivational effects, but once a stable sense of self-competence is developed they may become mere epiphenomena.

SEX DIFFERENCES AND THE PURSUIT OF SUCCESS

We have not yet admitted that an increasing feeling of unease developed along with the early nAch literature. Most studies had tended to use male subjects, but it was becoming quite clear that research predictions had a tendency to go awry when female subjects were used. With the advent of a more insistent voicing of feminist issues, such theoretical 'embarrassments' were transformed into a springboard for much of the creative research in this area to date.

The real-life facts, which any useful theory must ultimately address, are stark, although much is changing and some things are changing very fast. At every level of traditionally defined vocational and professonal achievement, women have taken second place to men. In the work environment, the majority of women have traditionally worked in 'women's occupations', which in turn have usually had less pay and prestige than those dominated by men. If women work alongside men in the same jobs they tend to advance less up the promotion ladder. Some of the reasons for this inequality are so obvious and unrelated to motivation that we need not dwell too long on them in this text. It is not too long ago that it was widely held that women were naturally inferior to men and would undoubtedly do less well if they had temerity enough to compete in a man's world. Blatant discrimination was till comparatively recently commonplace, and equal-rights legislation in western democracies can hardly be said to have abolished the problem.

Motivation researchers have been more interested in investigating subtler reasons for sex differences. Do women on average experience less need to achieve than men, regardless of opportunity? However, in posing that question, how broad a context do we allow achievement to operate in, given that much early nAch research could be accused of defining achievement in male terms? Are the motives to seek success or alternatively to avoid failure the only important motives that are engaged by achievement goals? These are important research questions which have very general relevance, even though they may have been largely prompted by the existence of sex differences.

Horner (1968) set the agenda for research into the existence of another achievement-related motive which supposedly had particular relevance to women. She claimed that achievement goals were capable of arousing a 'fear of success'. Why should anyone be afraid of succeeding? One possibility might be that success will interfere with the satisfaction of needs other than achievement ones. Maslow's hierarchy of motives is discussed elsewhere in this context: affiliation is mentioned by Maslow as an important class of needs. Need to feel loved by others, approved of by others, are powerful social motives in our society. Taken to excess they are thought by certain psychotherapists to lie at the core of many neurotic disorders (Ellis 1980). Horner believed that stereotyped views about the role of women in society may persuade many women that there is a success/likeability trade-off, such that success may lead to difficulty satisfying friendship and intimacy needs.

Since Horner first put forward this idea several problems have emerged. First of all Horner's projective test used to measure fear of success lacks reliability. More importantly, in so far as the concept has been measured, it appears that males often score as highly as females. Thus whenever succeeding may involve some unpopularity, which it sometimes but not always does, it seems that men and women show similar individual differences. Nowhere is the male need for approval more convincingly illustrated than in Dixon's (1976) informative book on the psychology of military incompetence. Generals of course have tended to a man to be men, and yet some of the worst cases of incompetence have been due to unrealistic need for social approval getting in the way of the need to achieve success. Society does of course make different demands on men and women, so different means of satisfying the need for approval have to be taken into account. But it is by no means certain that achievement needs and approval/affiliation needs are more in competition for females than males. The case is certainly even more dubious if we take an even wider view of achievement than a simply vocational one.

Sex differences in achievement may also be approached from the attribution theory framework that we have already discussed. There is some evidence (Eccles 1983) that females are less likely than males to attribute success internally, thus leading to less positive concepts of self-competence. Equally, they are more likely to attribute lack of success to lack of ability, thus further eroding feelings of competence. However, one must be careful not to exaggerate the magnitude of effect here. We must also bear in mind the hazardous status of attributions in explaining real behavioural differences in motivational variables. As for performance variables these can show a completely contrary pattern; for example, females may predict future performance less confidently than males but then do better on a task.

We have seen already that attributions, while not irrelevant to achievement-striving in the longer term, often serve a short-term retrospective role in enhancing or defending the ego, following success or failure experiences. There seems little doubt that here at least the male ego seems to require more bolstering. Interestingly the female-linked pattern of a lack of self-serving attribution has formed a part of cognitive formulations of depressive illness (Abramson, Seligman, and Teasdale 1978). Depression in turn affects women more than men.

Yet another approach to the question of sex differences lies in partitioning the traditional nAch construct into component parts. This has been the approach of Spence and Helmreich (1983). Using questionnaire techniques and factor analysis they have discovered three such components: work orientation, mastery, and competitiveness. Factor structure is the same for men and women, suggesting that we are dealing with the same over-all concept in both sexes. Sex differences in magnitude of scores on the three components were not great and largely confined to competitiveness, on which females score less highly. On tendency to work hard and do a good job (work orientation) females if anything scored slightly higher than males. All factors correlated modestly with endorsements of stereotypically masculine traits (such as independence, decisiveness) but they did not on the other hand correlate at all negatively with stereotypically feminine traits such as tact and empathy. In any event, despite the tendency for people to see masculinity and femininity as opposite ends of a pole, they are themselves unrelated dimensions: people can be high on so-called masculinity and at the same time high on so-called femininity. Thus Spence and Helmreich's results give no support to the view that achievement-needs necessarily get in the way of traditionally female concerns. We have already in any case suggested that females do not necessarily have a prerogative on the expression of affiliation needs, especially those concerned with social approval.

Spence and Helmreich's work does not so far tell us anything positive about real sex differences in achievement though it does cast doubt on some traditional views. Their work has paid dividends, however, in showing that the three components of nAch, as traditionally defined, do not all relate positively to achievement. In particular, in several different studies, they report that an interactive dimension of being high-scoring on work orientation and mastery but low-scoring on competitiveness gives the best prediction of real achievement. This pattern of results is shown for the salaries of businessmen in Figure 12.

Predictions have also been successfully made for the number of times academic scientists have had their publications cited by others, and most important, a prospective study showed that the measure

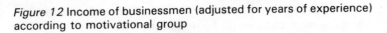

Figure 12 Income of businessmen (adjusted for years of experience) according to motivational group

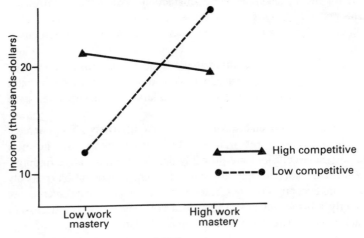

(After Spence and Helmreich 1983)

predicted academic grades achieved by students. While one would not want to rule out a positive role for competitiveness in some circumstances (sport perhaps?), these studies do show that it is often a significant drawback to achievement. The obvious reason behind such a harming effect is that achievement often needs the co-operation of others and competitiveness may serve only to alienate those around the person.

Helmreich *et al*. (1980) took on the interesting task of predicting — albeit retrospectively — the citations of academics. Using the technique of path analysis, they once again highlighted a stubborn sex difference: women scientists were cited less often than men. If citation can be taken as some measure of the worth of a researcher's publications, then why do women achieve less on this index? The use of path analysis and multiple regression by (Helmreich *et al*.) ruled out some of the obvious factors. Obviously multiple demands on women from family and job might lead to fewer publications and thus citations; since citations and publications related to the reputation of both graduate and current department, it could be that discrimination operated at these key selection points. However, even when these obvious variables are statistically controlled for, still the citation difference exists. The authors were forced to conclude that the reasons for the difference must be subtle. One possibility not investigated directly by the authors concerns the importance given to academic work in terms of an over-all value

127

system. Values rather than more superficial attitudes are seen by many psychologists as enduring guides to behaviour. Runge (1980) showed that for male academics work satisfaction most strongly correlated with general life satisfaction; leisure activities came second; quality of personal relationships came a poor third. For women academics good personal relationships were the most important determinant of general life satisfaction, although work satisfaction came a very close second. Thus the women academics could be seen as having the extra job of trying to keep two equally valued kites up in the air at the same time.

We have now seen how the topic of sex differences has generated much motivational research over the last decade or so. The most important conclusions are probably derived from negative findings. Women are not naturally lower in achievement motivation (possibly with the exception of competitiveness which as we have seen is not exactly a disadvantage). There does not seem to be any necessary antagonism between the satisfaction of affiliation needs and achievement needs which hampers women, except perhaps the point we have made latterly concerning the difficulties of spreading one's attention more thinly over more than one highly valued area of life satisfaction. Values indeed are probably the nub of the issue, since the prevailing values in a society will determine how it chooses to define achievement. While significant changes have occurred in society in regard to women 'competing' in a man's world, less change has occurred in regard to re-evaluations of what is primarily meant by achievement. The psychologist, *qua* scientific observer, will want no doubt to 'watch this space' for future and possibly hectic developments.

EXTRINSIC VERSUS INTRINSIC MOTIVATION

The notions of achievement motivation and intrinsic motivation are closely allied. Both imply working on some problem or in some area to bring about a sense of inner satisfaction at having succeeded. The goal is simply to do well, to achieve excellence. Often this state of affairs is contrasted with what is called extrinsic motivation, where one is working at a task, for example, not for its own sake but for the sake of some tangible externally provided reward which is known to follow successful completion. The obvious example of tangible reward in our society is the money that one earns from a job.

When we were discussing Atkinson's motivational theory, we

mentioned that in more recent versions extrinsic motivation is added to intrinsic as a possible extra variable determining a person's approach to tasks. Our society, by its system of carrot and stick, ensures that lack of intrinsic motivation is not sufficient reason to shy from the execution of certain tasks. However, two problems arise with regard to the distinction between extrinsic and intrinsic motivation. First the distinction itself is by no means as clear-cut as we have just implied. Second, in certain circumstances the two sources of motivation interact with each other rather than simply add together. We address each problem in turn. The first is highlighted by looking at motivation and the world of work.

MOTIVATION AT WORK

Maslow's ideas about human motivation were put forward at just the right time to be highly influential in the growing area of occupational psychology. After the Second World War, employees were to become at a premium, and employers, no doubt for other enlightened reasons too, began to ask how, other than through the pay-packet, could workers find greater satisfaction in their jobs. The employers' self-interest in this question was the assumption that employer loyalty and productivity would flow from greater job satisfaction. Maslow's theory predicts that as material needs are satisfied by adequate pay, so other needs such as affiliative needs and achievement needs seek greater expression. Managers were soon talking the language of job enrich-ment schemes along with their psychological consultants. Such schemes would be designed to fulfil these high level needs.

An influential theory of work motivation in particular was put forward by Herzberg (1966). In it he distinguishes between so-called satisfiers and dissatisfiers. These roughly parallel intrinsic motivators and extrinsic respectively. Thus monetary earnings are extrinsic and their presence does no more than ensure that dissatisfaction is avoided. Job enrichment factors when introduced affect intrinsic motivation and directly push up job satisfaction. The theory has been criticized on many grounds, not least empirical ones: job enrichment schemes often failed to have predicted effects on productivity. However, it is the methodological flaws which are most relevant to our point of discussion.

The essence of the matter is that every tangible incentive offered by an employer can be interpreted as either an intrinsic or an extrinsic factor. Money, the superficially most obvious extrinsic incentive, can be seen as a symbol of status, or a mark of recognition of one's value to the company. Both of these could be seen as serving to increase intrinsic motivation: the money's material value is taken as subordinate to its symbolic role in signalling the success which is sought for its own sake. On the other hand some non-monetary pat on the back for one's efforts which ordinarily may be thought of as fostering intrinsic motivation, can be interpreted extrinsically if it seems that job performance is not valued for its own sake but only *en route* to satisfying a strong need for approval. Just as surely as with money, job performance then becomes merely a means to an end. Thus applied psychologists interested in motivation are forced to concern themselves with the likely interpretation of incentive schemes and changes in working conditions, looked at against the particular applied context under consideration. Having issued that caveat, we ask: Are there any important differences between the way extrinsic and intrinsic motivation functions? This question itself has two important aspects: motivational effects which help determine such things as satisfaction, interest, persistence, etc., and motivational effects on quality and/or quantity of performance, output, etc. Although the two are often related, their linkage is in the final analysis itself a matter for empirical investigation.

THE INTERACTION OF EXTRINSIC AND INTRINSIC MOTIVATION

We distinguish here between extrinsic reward conditions, where performance at a task or on a job leads to some material reward, and intrinsic reward conditions where no external reward is offered for performance except that accruing to the person by dint of their own pride in doing the job well. (We shall also remain aware of the possible importance, mentioned above, of the symbolic functions of externally given rewards.)

There is a great deal of evidence from controlled laboratory experiments that provision of a reward for carrying out some task can sometimes have a deleterious effect on performance (see Lepper and Greene 1978). Moreover there is a reasonable litmus test for deciding whether performance on a particular task will show improvement or impairment as a result of offering reward — usually a small monetary incentive offered to student volunteer subjects. In many tasks good performance can result from the correct application of an algorithm — a rule — which when followed guarantees success, or it can come from a heuristic approach (see below). In the most boring of tasks an algorithm may be self-evident in the instructions for the task itself, for example 'Cancel all the letter *es* that you see as you scan a page of text.' In other tasks the solution may require a slightly more complex carrying out of a series of information processing and executive decisions, for example, 'If the coloured light and the tone occur together press button B.' All such tasks, however, share a rather uncreative common denominator: rule-following leads to success. The difference between good and bad performance is likely to be restricted to optimizing speed and accuracy in carrying out formal operations.

However, in other tasks the use of algorithm is contrasted with a use of so-called heuristic — the setting up as it were of a number of what might be temporary hypotheses, trying each out until a correct solution to the problem is obtained. Obviously this is a more creative endeavour which comes into its own when an obvious solution to a task problem is not apparent.

This heuristic/algorithmic distinction then helps us to predict whether extrinsic reward facilitates or hinders on-task performance. On the whole, laboratory studies tend to confirm that creative problem-solving tasks which involve heuristic strategies can be hindered by external reward, whereas algorithmic routine tasks may well be helped. There is another aspect to the litmus test, however, which overlaps this distinction: extrinsic rewards often have their counter-productive effects when the level of interest, and therefore presumably intrinsic reward, is already high. This of course is to suggest that extrinsic reward can indeed interact with, rather than simply add to, intrinsic motivation. This intrinsic interest dimension overlaps with the heuristic/algorithmic dimension in the sense that routine tasks are often seen as lacking in interest, whereas those involving some creative solution often engage interest.

The really important question of course is why these performance effects are sometimes obtained. There are two explanations which are not necessarily mutually exclusive. The first harks back to our chapter on arousal theory. Regardless of our final stance on arousal theory, we did learn that certain so-called arousers have been linked in systematic ways to deleterious effects on task performance. One such arouser that has been researched is extrinsic incentive. The mechanism which in turn links high arousal to worsened performance probably involves attentional effects. Many arousers are known to cause attention to be more narrowly focused on some central aspect of a task. This might of course help in the speedy execution of some routine task, but may hinder more creative endeavour.

This sort of argument has led some to question in some instances the use, in behaviour modification programmes, of 'tokens' (exchangeable for material rewards) in shaping new learning. The fear, realistic or not, is that token rewards may lead to token learning. However, such easy speculation has not in general helped the development of research in this area (see Quattrone 1985). Some caution may be justified if highly arousing incentives are offered for correct solutions of complex heuristic tasks. Subjects may indeed concentrate so single-mindedly on getting the correct solution for immediate gain that they do not explore and find out about the problem in depth. Reward contingency may encourage superficiality. However, this probably does not have any bearing on the major area of application for behaviour modification programmes using tokens. Moreover, the phenomenon of extrinsic reward detracting from performance depends on intrinsic reward and natural interest being already present; behaviour modification programmes are most often introduced when self-initiated behaviour is nil. Indeed it can be argued that such programmes, artificial as they may appear at the outset, are often successful in allowing people to experience intrinsic rewards for behaviour not previously shown. Certainly any designer of a behaviour modification programme who claimed any degree of professional training would be well aware of the eventual necessity of fading out extrinsic rewards artificially given and letting intrinsic motivation take over, helped perhaps by periodic pats on the back from (if possible) a responsive environment.

The essence of the arousal-based theory of performance impairment is that incentives can themselves sometimes be so arousing that cognitive functioning itself is impaired. The second explanation for the impairment suggests that the addition of extrinsic rewards diminishes intrinsic motivation. The detailed argument brings us back to a consideration of attribution theory.

We have seen that 'causal' attributions lie at the heart of attribution theory. People are assumed to behave like would-be scientists, forever seeking the causes of their own and others' behaviour. Earlier in the chapter we were concerned with people's attributions for success and failure. Here we are concerned with their attributions about why they are doing what they are doing at any time. The crucial attributional dimension is again the internal/external dimension of locus of control. We can either believe we are doing X for its own sake, in which case the behaviour is internally driven, as it were, or we can believe that we are merely doing X as a means to an end, a reward for example — in which case we may feel that our behaviour is being controlled by external factors: we would not be doing X except that we have to in order to get Y. So much for initial assumptions. The next line of argument also echoes Weiner's views discussed earlier. Intrinsic motivation is identified with making internal attributions for our behaviour and making internal attributions is part and parcel of feeling good. There are also echoes of chapter 7 and the need to feel in control of events. Different theorists (Lepper and Greene 1978; Deci 1975) have different ways of putting the argument but the essentials can be summed up in the view of the educational philosopher, A.S. Neil, cited by Morgan (1982): the promise of a reward communicates the expectation that the rewarded task was not otherwise worth doing. For theorists such as Deci (1975) we may add that finding oneself doing too much for external rewards encourages self-perception of being controlled by them, which in turn vitiates feelings of self efficacy and competence.

What happens then when we add extrinsic reward to intrinsic? People ask themselves why they are carrying out the task. Where before interest alone justified behaviour, we can now suppose that people see their behaviour as being over-justified. Attribution theory then goes on to assume that the agent resolves this surfeit of justifications by discounting the importance of the previous interest. In short, interest and intrinsic motivation is diminished, and with it (perhaps) the quality or quantity of performance. How good is the theory?

It certainly predicts quite well the circumstances in which we get decreases in apparent interest in a task. There have been sufficient experiments done to allow us to talk about a genuine replicable effect. We will illustrate this by reference to two typical experiments: one by Lepper and Greene using children as subjects; and one by Deci, using students.

In both studies an experimental group of subjects is rewarded for performance on a task which previously has been shown to be intrinsically interesting. In the case of Lepper and Greene, the children performed a drawing task; in Deci's experiment, subjects solved puzzles. The final procedural step is to take a measure of interest in the activity after the rewarded session. Deci pretended to leave his subjects alone for a while afterwards, but in fact observed the extent to which subjects continued to work on the puzzles. Lepper and Greene observed the children's choice of the drawing game in a later free play session. In both cases the experimental subjects showed less interest afterwards than control subjects who had not been offered any reward.

Further experimentation confirms the pattern of results, but what has seriously concerned the attention of reviewers (Morgan 1982; Quattrone 1985) has been the embarrassing lack of evidence to show that attributional changes underlie the correctly predicted effects. Quattrone at least sees the embarrassments as perhaps more apparent than real.

First, many of the cases in which assumed attributional effects are not in line with prediction (but behaviour is) have utilized young children as subjects. There are serious methodological problems when it comes to inferences about children's mental processes. There are far less inconsistencies in experiments with older subjects.

Second, we can reiterate the point we made earlier about the importance of the interpretation that is given to an external reward. In one of Deci's experiments, for example, the role of verbal praise was looked at. A pronounced sex difference was found in its effects. It seemed that male subjects 'interpreted' the praise as a 'symbol' that they were doing well — it thus did not reduce intrinsic interest. It seemed that the female subjects interpreted praise as an extrinsic 'approval' reward, which did reduce intrinsic interest. Although that is by no means the only interpretation of Deci's results, it does fit in with a general finding that rewards which are seen as highly contingent on performance and therefore interpretable as informative feedback are less likely to produce 'discounting', while reward which amounts to mere bribery to participate is most likely to produce 'discounting'. Thus perception that extrinsic motivation is involved in performance may be necessary for discounting to take place; it is not sufficient.

Third, whether a subject's intrinsic interest is impaired by extrinsic reward must also depend on the initial level of interest. It is not surprising that loss of interest occurs most reliably in experiments where a mere modicum of interest is present. No one has demonstrated waning of interest as a result of offering competition prizes to committed hobby enthusiasts.

In fact we might wish to conclude this discussion of attribution theory as we did the last. No doubt attributions play a role in developing intrinsic motivation as we assumed they also played a role in developing self-competence and expectancies about achievement. They probably play little immediate causative role in determining day-to-day levels of intrinsic motivation, except in some highly specific situations.

CONCLUSION

In this chapter we have looked at a number of key motivational phenomena concerning the way we go about seeking (or indeed avoiding) various goals. Although the structure of the chapter has often concentrated on achievement goals, we have seen that many more motives than simply a need for achievement are involved. Interpreted widely so as to include any challenging situation where success and failure outcomes are salient, it is possible to see an array of personal and social motives being involved. As in many areas the recent trend has been to generate cognitive theories of motivational phenomena. The reader may judge the extent to which successful achievement has been the result of this endeavour.

10

Affect, emotion, and cognition

We left emotion at the end of chapter 6 in a state of 'becoming'. Simple physiological theories such as those of James and Lange were shown to be inadequate. The famous experiment by Schachter and Singer (1962) turned out to be more noteworthy for the push it gave to increasingly cognitive ways of looking at emotion than for the definitiveness of its findings. In this chapter we examine further the more recent 'cognitivization' of emotion; we shall see that arguments about the role of cognition in emotion reflect conceptual confusion as much as genuine differences of opinion. If indeed linguistic philosophers wished to identify the one area of psychology which they would find most tiresome it would probably be the area of emotion. For reasons that will become apparent as this chapter develops, I have chosen to include the additional word 'affect' to share pride of place in the chapter heading.

Schachter's hypothesis was that arousal and cognitions (drawn from the social context) are both necessary components of an emotion. The arousal, as it were, gives guts to the emotion. The cognition tells us what exactly the guts are being given to. I deliberately use this 'hot' language description so that we can contrast this position with the next bit of cognitivization that took place. In a series of experiments, Valins introduced a methodology based on giving false feedback of heart rate to subjects. In doing so, Valins was making a cognitive take-over bid for the entire emotion construct by suggesting that a person does not actually need veridical knowledge of gut arousal, through, for example, heart rate. Instead the person 'coldly' assesses information about external social context and internal bodily arousal. The experiments aimed to give support to this view.

Thus snake phobic subjects were shown to show less subsequent avoidance if they were led to believe that their heart rates were not affected by snake slides but were affected by other anxiety-arousing slides (Valins and Ray 1967). In another experiment it was claimed that degree of sexual attraction to nude pin-ups could be influenced by the same technique of false feedback.

Despite what some see as their ingenuity, these experiments can be criticized on a number of grounds. Methodologically Valins and his co-workers did not measure real heart-rate, so it was perfectly possible that the false feedback of heart rate influenced real heart rate in these experiments; there is certainly evidence that false feedback can influence real arousal and thence emotional responding (Hirschmann 1975). Attempts to replicate Valins's work have either been unsuccessful or the effects weak. Perhaps the major criticism of the experiments is seen in what exactly was affected: in the one case snake-approach behaviour, in the other case attractiveness ratings. In other words there is no evidence that emotional feelings have been manipulated. How did subjects interpret what must have appeared a bizarre experiment? Was their crucial behaviour really influenced by some assumed emotional mediation or could it have been due to some other characteristics of the set-up which led subjects to think that they should behave in a certain way? Even if the behavioural effects are assumed to reflect emotional mediation, it is worth repeating that the effects are weak. We may note that false feedback has not entered the phobia clinic as a great therapy method. Some have concluded their assessment of the false-feedback literature by suggesting that we see such studies as affecting something called 'secondary' emotion as opposed to 'primary' emotion (see Taylor *et al.* 1982). Primary emotion is emotion with the guts left in. An alternative strategy is to refuse to call such artificial effects emotional at all.

The question of what is an emotion is indeed the central question. The answer which might best be given before all others is that it is a word in the English language, and like any word its meaning is defined by its use, and in this particular case the psychologist should take Wittgenstein's comments on definition to heart: for example, a table is not a table because it has any one particular feature which captures the essence of 'tableness', rather it shares a reasonable sufficiency of family resemblances with an existing family of things which a linguistic community has decided to call tables. What then of emotion?

A search of *Roget's Thesaurus* will result in a list of several tens of 'states' all with a claim to be called emotions; many will overlap but the list would include a cornucopia of diversity. How then could we expect to keep the meaning of the ordinary word 'emotion' and expect to pin down some necessary common feature? Rather than corrupt and restrict the perfectly useful meaning of the English language term, psychologists would be better advised to make their own more rigorous terminological distinctions when talking about states as diverse as: affection, anger, anguish, anxiety, awe, benevolence, boredom, contempt, depression, disgust, disillusionment, distress, dread, elation, enjoyment, enthusiasm, envy, exhuberance, fear, grief, guilt, hate, ill-will, indignation, irritation, jealousy, joy, longing, love, lust, panic, pathos, pity, pride, rage, regret, remorse, reverence, sadness, shame, sorrow, surprise, tenderness, terror, vanity, wonder, wrath (list taken from M.B. Arnold and cited in Harré 1983).

And yet one of the liveliest exchanges on the role of cognition in emotion (I refer to Zajonc versus Lazarus in the *American Psychologist* 1984) seems to draw all its liveliness from conceptual confusions of the sort 'all emotion involves cognition'. Clearly it all depends on whether the latter is taken as analytic (that is, a matter of definition) or synthetic (open to empirical investigation). That this seems to be realized to some extent by both parties suggests that adversarial glee informs the debate more than genuine differences of opinion. If Lazarus wishes, as he seems, to say that all emotion requires cognition as a precondition and to make that statement analytic, then the question is not whether he is doing something which is correct but rather whether he is doing anything useful for a specialized community of scholars. By excluding as emotional phenomena such things as the showing of sensory preferences he does seem to be restricting the ordinary language umbrella of things emotional, as well as side-stepping some of the evidence ranged against him by Zajonc. It is notable that the title of Zajonc's paper is 'On the primacy of affect'. For Lazarus much of affect is not emotion; it has to be so otherwise Zajonc wins. And yet Zajonc has the Oxford English Dictionary on his side, since affect is defined as feeling, emotion, desire. But if affect is emotion then with regard to what has affect got primacy? If the logic of the debate is its worst feature the issues addressed are its best feature. Both Zajonc and Lazarus separately highlight different but useful perspectives on emotion, which we can further explore in this chapter.

THE UNIVERSALITY OF EMOTIONAL EXPRESSION

Although this issue is not directly relevant to the assessment of the role of cognition in emotion, it is certainly important to know whether for some emotions at least there is a cross-cultural consensus in the way that separate emotions are expressed and communicated. The principal expressive medium is of course the human face. There is now sufficient accumulated evidence from studies by researchers such as Ekman, Izard, and many others to say that the following emotions have a universal facial expression: happiness, anger, disgust, sadness, and a combined notion of fear/surprise (see Ekman and Oster 1982 for a full review of pertinent studies).

The common research technique has been to show subjects from different cultures series of emotion-expressing facial photographs, and record the amount of cross-cultural agreement. Using this technique agreement is high even when the people in the photographs are from a different cultural and racial group. It is also important to note that the evidence obtained holds good for preliterate as well as literate cultures. It cannot therefore be maintained that high agreement rates are due to shared learning experiences involving common exposure to mass media representations of emotional expression.

Given then that certain emotions do have universal means of facial expression, it is certainly possible that these emotions are hard-wired reactions which initially could be linked fairly reflexively to the perception of a limited range of stimuli. This is Zajonc's position. Cognitive elaboration might take place as a result of individual development but initially at least the emotional reactions occur without what Lazarus would term cognitive appraisal. This is Zajonc's and Izard's (1984) argument for 'ontogenetic primacy' of emotion over cognition. Incidentally it is easy to exemplify the nature of the gulf between Zajonc and Lazarus on just this sort of point: when a newly born infant reacts to a nasty taste with the facial expression of 'disgust', Zajonc is tempted to call it the full emotion, which later can become linked to the appraisal of more complex situations; Lazarus prefers to label the facial expression as a gustofacial response. Since adults also use the word 'disgust' in relation to their feelings about tastes and smells, when, we may ask, will Lazarus allow a gustofacial response to become an emotional response? If the answer is 'never' because expressions of sensory likes and dislikes are not emotions then Lazarus in this case seems singularly to be clouding the issue of how we come to use the same word in the presence of a taste or smell and to describe the emotion we feel when we read, say, a particularly 'tasteless' article in the gutter press. He also would appear to be ignoring a certain etymological linkage. On this same point it is ironic that Lazarus curiously cites Tomkins (1982) as having 'explicitly excluded pain and pleasure from the category of emotions'. First of all the citation seems perversely to misunderstand Tomkins, who is quite clear in his list of nine 'innate' affects to differentiate positive and negative groupings. By which he means what if not pleasureable and painful emotions? Second, in the same article Tomkins himself writes: 'It is my view that theories (e.g. Arnold or Lazarus) that postulate such appraisal as a necessary condition for affect activation are more embarrassed by unlearned activation than my theory is embarrassed by the learned activation of affect.'

Affect or emotion? The reader should feel free to use the terms according to his or her own convenience. Meanwhile our chapter title aims for inclusivity in what is ultimately of importance: the range of phenomena addressed. We shall first address phenomena in the field of emotion which appear to involve little if any cognitive appraisal processes.

AFFECTIVE REACTIONS ESTABLISHED WITHOUT COGNITIVE APPRAISAL

First of all we can mention some of the findings which Zajonc ranges against Lazarus, which are telling unless either emotion is defined to exclude them or the term cognitive appraisal is so widened as to be assumed in virtually every reaction. If we wish to remain neutral as between Zajonc and Lazarus then we can say simply that there are some interesting affective reactions which would appear to involve minimal cognitive appraisal.

Affective reactions to tastes can be classically conditioned — not in itself a fact that rules out cognition. However, an experiment by Garcia and Rusiniak (1980) demonstrated that successful conditioning can occur even when the unconditioned stimulus is administered and has its effect while an animal is under anaesthesia. Thus a certain food (CS) can come to be associated with nausea, even though the nauseous agent (US) is presented and has its effect during an unconscious state.

Equally at an unconscious level, affective preferences can be established for stimuli even though the stimuli are presented in such degraded form that they defy recognition by the subject (Seamon *et al.* 1983). Interestingly preferences were better established for stimuli presented to the right visual field. Another early but fascinating study (Littman and Manning 1954) showed that smokers could not identify their own brand of cigarette in blind tests, if simply asked to do so; if, however, they were asked which they liked the best they tended to pick out their own brand.

One area of research on affect, highly relevant to any book on motivation and emotion, is only fleetingly referred to in Zajonc's article. This is R.L. Solomon's opponent process theory of acquired motivation. Zajonc confines his remarks to saying that Lazarus's views on the necessity of appraisal 'would play havoc' with the theory. Lazarus chooses not to answer this particular point. Solomon's theory, in any event, demands more detailed consideration. In the opinion of at least this author, it represents undervalued equity on the stock exchange of psychological theories.

OPPONENT-PROCESS THEORY

The notion that pain follows pleasure and pleasure follows pain is hardly a new idea. It is central, as Solomon (1980) notes, to the philosophical bases of most historical episodes of puritanism. The writer Anon long ago contributed this barbed comment on the consequences of making love: *post coitum omne animal triste est*. Universally true it may not be but it serves as a suitable introduction to Solomon's theory.

When some affectively arousing stimulus occurs repeatedly the theory says that we can observe three important phenomena: hedonic contrast, habituation, and withdrawal. Although the theory is a theory of acquired motivation — how we come to be powerfully motivated to seek originally unsought goals — Solomon makes it quite clear that 'in every case of acquired motivation, affective or hedonic processes are involved', and that it is these three affective phenomena which can account for much acquired motivation.

Let us look first at the contrast phenomenon. If a moving mother duck is presented for the first time to a neonatal duckling, the result is that an affectively neutral state changes to one of excitement, keeping the mother in sight and stumbling in her direction. When the mother is removed, very quickly the duckling, far from returning to the neutral baseline, shows instead the typical distress calling of its species. Similarly, if a newly born baby, not yet wanting or needing externally derived nutrients, is nevertheless introduced to a bottle nipple, sucking will ensue. If after a minute the bottle is removed, once again

141

crying and signs of distress are evident. Should we be surprised by these findings? Certainly we should find certain features of the two cases interesting. First of all the opposing affective reaction that follows the removal of the first stimulus has had no opportunity to be learned; second, as Solomon himself points out, it is possible that the duckling or infant could never have experienced the second negative affective state by any known variety of direct stimulation. Third, whatever appraisal processes might be involved in eliciting the primary affect, the secondary affect that follows would appear to be totally automatic; this is the implication of Zajonc's reference mentioned earlier.

The theory believes that hedonic contrast occurs as a general rule whenever affect is aroused: in short a primary affect ('A' state) gives rise to a secondary and opposite affect ('B' state). Nor does the A state have to be pleasurable and the B state aversive. Sauna baths usually start off by being painfully searing experiences, which, when they are over, give rise to pleasurable after-glows; euphoric feelings often follow in the wake of the terror that precedes a first parachute jump, etc. The automaticity of the A-B sequence parallels what we know about opponent processes in colour perception: turn on a red light, stare at it and see how its redness becomes less intense as a minute goes by; now turn it off and quite automatically you will see a green after-image which only slowly dies away.

Hedonic habituation refers to the tendency for affective A reactions to decline in intensity with repeated presentations of the affective arouser. We shall see shortly that the degree of habituation (as well as the degree of hedonic withdrawal) depends on exactly what is meant by repeated presentations. The duration between presentations is a critical variable. Meanwhile the reader may well be able to see the relevance of opponent-process theory to what is possibly the most powerful source of acquired motivation, namely drug addiction. Solomon's notion of habituation is synonymous with the notion of 'tolerance'. Higher doses of a drug, more dangerous thrills (spicier food?), all become more necessary to evoke the same intensity of the A state.

Meanwhile, with repeated presentations, affective withdrawal also takes place. Just as the A state weakens with use, so does the B state strengthen. In the case of addiction, the term 'withdrawal symptoms' is of course used to describe just this intensification of aversive B state following the withdrawal of drug effects. But the theory predicts similarly for pleasurable B states: with experience the painful aspects of a sauna bath should lessen (habituate) while the pleasurable feelings that follow should intensify. Similarly with increasing experience of parachute jumping, pre-jump terror should change to something like nervous but thrilling anticipation, while post-jump stunned relief should change to more long lasting euphoria.

The theoretical basics of opponent-process theory are diagrammatized in Figure 13. A states have short latency, build up to their peak rapidly and then rapidly decline when stimulation ceases. By contrast B states have longer latency, slower build up and slower decay. If we assume that each process is inaugurated at the time of affective arousal, and if we assume that both component profiles are summed to produce a manifest experienced affect then we get the final profile typical of Solomon's predictions. Note also how with repeated activation of the system the intensity of the experienced A state weakens, whereas both the intensity and duration of the B state increases.

Figure 13 Summation of 'A' and 'B' processes for familiar and novel stimulation

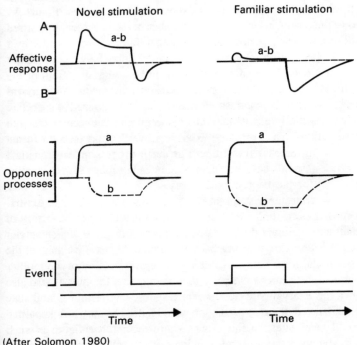

(After Solomon 1980)

143

So much for the theory and anecdotal evidence. What is much more impressive is some of the experimental evidence adduced in its support. Space limits us to considering only a small portion of such evidence but a comprehensive review is offered by Solomon (1980). If we stay with the ducklings mentioned earlier, we can see in an experiment by Starr (1978) that the idea of habituation and withdrawal being related to a 'critical decay duration' between repetitions of A state arousal achieves quantitative expression. We saw that removal of the mother causes distress calling. Habituation and withdrawal principles should ensure that repeated presentations and removals of the mother figure should increase the intensity and duration of the B state (distress calling), as long as the interval between presentations is not so long as to allow the opponent process to decay rather than build up. In Starr's experiment all ducklings were exposed to a mother figure for six minutes in all. Different groups of ducklings were however given different patterns of exposure. The three experimental groups each received twelve thirty-second exposures but with different time intervals between repetitions: one, two, or five minutes. Finally a control group received just one exposure of six minutes. Figure 14 shows the results in terms of mean number of seconds spent in distress calling after each removal of the mother figure.

Note that with the longest, five minute, delay between presentations of the mother figure there seems to be no buildup at all of the B process: distress calling is much the same after the twelfth removal as after the first. By contrast, distress calling is maximized in the group which has the minimal interval of one minute between successive presentations. Thus repeated exposures over a short period of time do seem to increase the strength of the B process unless a critical interval — in this case less than 5 minutes but more than 2 minutes — is left for the B process to decay.

An operant theorist might of course suggest that in this experiment distress calling itself functioned not just as a passive affective reaction to removal, but as an active operant response which served after a little delay to bring back the mother figure: in other words distress calling is being reinforced by re-presentation of the mother figure. Since there is evidence that operant conditioning is stronger when the interval between operant response and reinforcer delivery is not delayed, then the prediction would indeed be that distress calling would be greatest in the group where the mother figure is most immediately reintroduced following distress calling, that is, the one minute interval group. This alternative interpretation however fails

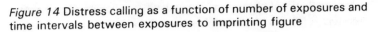

Figure 14 Distress calling as a function of number of exposures and time intervals between exposures to imprinting figure

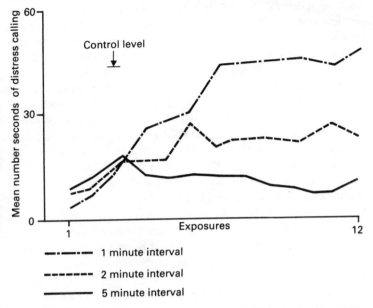

Note the lack of growth of the opponent process when 5 minutes elapsed between exposures.
(After Starr 1978)

to explain the data obtained from the control group, which does not have twelve operant learning trials as it were. In this group the 'B' process as predicted increases during the prolonged continuous six-minute exposure and distress calling is at the same level as the one-minute interval group achieves at the end of twelve exposures.

Other laboratory findings have demonstrated measurable 'savings' effects in opponent process activation. Thus when an A process is rested for a few days, the B process virtually disappears; but when trials recommence, the B process is restrengthened in less time than before. This of course tallies with clinical and anecdotal reports that readdiction to cigarettes or alcohol takes place very rapidly even after — or perhaps one should say especially after — long periods of abstinence.

The relevance of opponent-process theory to the development of addictive behaviour is obvious, and seems particularly to follow the theoretical predictions in view of such immediate and intense A processes being initially involved. Solomon's theory however is far more than a theory of addiction — or rather it invites us to see many

145

other motivational phenomena as paralleling addiction; social motives involving affiliation for example. Suppose you have an elderly relative who, being immobile, welcomes your occasional visits. The theory predicts that, above a certain level of visiting, the pleasure shown by your relative during your visits will diminish. Not surprising perhaps, since you will in common parlance have lost some of your novelty value. The theory also predicts, however, that your relative will develop a craving for your visits during your absence and the increasing strength of the craving will be in direct proportion to the waning of satisfaction during your visits. For the interested reader opponent-process theory has also been used to dissect the mechanics of love (Peele and Brodsky 1977).

Solomon is among the first to admit that his theory, for all its attractions, makes him a little worried. It is a wide-ranging theory meant, as we have seen, to make predictions across a wide spectrum of derived motives. Such theories are not currently in fashion, in an age where nearly everything, including theories, is 'mini' if not 'micro'. However, fashionability cannot be a serious objection to a theory. More of consequence are the complexities often involved in testing its predictions.

Like any phenomenon whose critical elements involve alternate time intervals, it is often not clear when exactly processes should be in evidence. Solomon's experimental evidence is clear for certain illustrative cases, but is the B process, for example, always at its peak soon after (in terms of the process's over-all duration) the eliciting stimulus for the A state is withdrawn? How soon is soon? And in cases not involving strict terminations such as an electric shock or parachute jump, when does the A state actually disappear? These crucial time interval lengths will no doubt vary from situation to situation and person to person, so the theory can only give guidance and encourage reasonable belief that if enough empirical investigation is done for a specific case then the principles of opponent-process theory will be found to be in evidence. Thus the theory is not unfalsifiable, it is just that the absolute values of its parameters can vary a great deal from situation to situation, since the theory only makes predictions about the patterning and relative strengths of the processes.

The same sort of difficulty applies to other aspects of the theory, notably the critical decay duration. There is no doubt that such a notion was given support in Starr's experiment. The notion also seems to ring true in implying that a number of occasional uses of a potentially addictive substance taken over a long time period will not engender the same degree of aversive craving and ultimately total addiction as the same number of uses concentrated into a short period of time. However, what exactly the critical decay duration is in any and every case remains an empirical matter to be ferreted out.

Another unanswered question in opponent-process theory is just what affective states can function as A or B processes. It has been suggested for example that certain emotional states which are always evoked by specific environmental happenings, such as grief, can only occur as A states. This might also be the case for depressed affect (see Ranieri and Zeiss 1984). However, there may be some reason to believe from studies looking at the effects of affect on memory and perception (see below) that opponent processes might be involved in certain cases of depressed mood induction (Blaney 1986; also Bray: personal communication).

One final question which needs addressing is the evolutionary significance of opponent-process theory. We can speculate that affect, like any disturbance of equilibrium, may be subject to some homeostatic regulation where over-shoot is a necessary part of a restoration process. A more fully worked-out evolutionary context would provide opponent-process theory with even greater plausibility than it already has.

THE INFLUENCE OF AFFECT ON COGNITIVE PROCESSES

Regardless of the definitional tangles of whether affect and emotion in some sense are or involve cognitions, it seems certainly to be the case that affect or emotional state influences cognitive processes, particularly memory processes. The dominant theoretical approach which brings together research in this area is that of Bower (1981). In a sense it does involve treating different affects and emotions as quasi-cognitions: for example Bower states that 'each specific emotion has a specific node or unit in memory . . . linked with propositions describing events from one's life during which that emotion was aroused'. Affect nodes are connected with all other nodes in a semantic network through which activation can spread. The theory can be seen as consistent with and elaborating on Tomkins's view of emotion as having an automatic and non-motivated amplifying effect on respond-ing (see Tomkins 1982), if by responding we include cognitive activity such as selective retrieval of memories which are congruent with the emotion elicited and therefore occupying nearby nodes in semantic memory.

There are in fact two sorts of finding which would be consistent

147

with Bower's model: state dependence and mood congruence. By the former we mean that what we learn while in a certain mood will be best recalled while in the same mood. Thus, if state dependence does occur for mood states, students ideally should practise their revision of examination material in as anxious an emotional state as is going to be the case when they have to retrieve it in the examination room. In the case of anxiety we are aware from research reviewed elsewhere in this book that the above strategy may be something less than ideal. More to the point there seems to be little evidence in general for state dependence effects in relation to mood states (Blaney 1986). Mood congruence is a different matter.

Mood congruence effects on memory processes depend not only on the supposed mood of the person. They also depend on the affective content of the material to be retrieved. Thus subjects in a positive hedonic mood should show a bias towards retrieving material with positive hedonic associations, whereas subjects in a negative hedonic mood should show a bias towards retrieving material with negative hedonic associations. Investigators have used a variety of techniques to test such predictions, so fortunately the pooling of strengths and cancelling out of weaknesses enables us to say that quite a lot of evidence points to the existence of genuine mood congruence effects.

It has long been known that depressed patients tend to selectively recall sadder life-episodes than control subjects. This kind of study however is particularly weak in regard to unequivocal demonstration of mood congruency effects, even though such studies are consistent with cognitive theories of depression, which emphasize the importance of biased cognitive processing in causing and then maintaining episodes of depressive illness (Beck 1974). First of all depressed patients may really differ from controls in the frequency of unhappy episodes in their life. Second, some other difference between depressed patients and controls may account for differential retrieval.

A different strategy gets round the first problem, although the second is unavoidable when comparing two independent groups where mood itself has not been manipulated. Depressed subjects can be compared with non-depressed subjects on the recall of experimentally induced events of positive (success) and negative (failure) affective quality. For example, Johnson *et al.* (1983) used groups of depressed and non-depressed undergraduates and got them to recall the content of tasks which they either had previously managed to finish successfully or had left unfinished. Depressed subjects, as expected, recalled more 'failure' tasks. Readers will recall that this is the same Zeigarnik effect procedure used by Atkinson and his colleagues to test predictions about achievement motivation. It would be interesting to speculate about the mediating role of affective processes in determining the pattern of their results.

Other studies have tried by a variety of means to manipulate mood itself and make it into a genuine independent variable. Techniques to induce depressed or elated mood states have included hypnosis, listening to music, reading mood-related statements, and success or failure manipulations. The results of approximately thirty such studies are reviewed by Blaney (1986). Although the over-all results suggest that mood congruence is a genuine phenomenon, the evidence is still unclear on a number of fronts. Because it is often difficult to assign absolute values to the positivity or negativity of both stimulus material and mood states, studies tend to agree only on the matter of findings being in a generally sensible direction; in regard to specifics, however, depressed mood subjects may recall fewer positive items or they may recall more negative items than elated subjects, depending on the study. What exactly would constitute a neutral control state is debatable: there is some reason to believe that normal states, rather than being neutral, are positive with regard to likely congruence effects, while depressed states involve a drift away from a positive recall bias to neutral rather more than a definite selective bias to negative material (see Blaney 1986: 238). Another problem of mood congruence is that no study so far seems to have demonstrated the quantitative prediction that degree of congruence effects is related to degree of mood induction. This could mean of course that only a certain threshold-reaching mood-shift is necessary for effects to occur. Equally, however, it could suggest that the manipulations of mood are having other effects (almost certainly this will be the case) and some aspect of these non-mood-related effects is causing the congruence phenomenon.

Cognitive theory in this area is recognizably in a state of infancy, and needs much development in spelling out its predictions and much more precision in specifying its variables. For example, 'priming' is often referred to as an alternative explanation of mood-congruence effects, although it is often far from clear a priori what would constitute evidence for or against the occurrence of 'priming'. Conclusions are often drawn about rarefied variables such as hedonic tone of stimuli, which may amount to a collection of words with pleasant or unpleasant connotations. Statistical analysis, let alone conclusions, will often depend on considering just what logical classes of entities are represented and by what sort of sampling procedure. If something like network theory should be seen as a crude starting position rather than a refined end-point, then it stands to reason that it cannot yet serve as an adequate basis for theories of affective disorders such as depression (see Power and Champion 1986 for a more detailed exposition of this thesis). At most we can say that there is some experimental evidence which illuminates some of the notions which have long been part of traditional cognitive theories of depression such as that of Beck. But even this statement needs qualification.

The finding mentioned above that depressed people tend to move away from positive selective bias but not necessarily towards outright negative bias is actually, as Blaney himself points out, against the Beckian stereotype of the depressed person as full of negative thoughts. One is reminded here of the results of another experiment (Alloy and Abramson 1979) carried out to test the predictions of Seligman's cognitive learning theory of depression, which predicts that depressives will underestimate the degree of control they have over certain important events. There was a difference found between depressives and normal controls, but it was the normals who overestimated degree of control rather than depressives who underestimated. It seems that depressives simply lack rose-tinted spectacles, which keep most people comfortably deluded about their self-efficacy.

A recurrent theme in different parts of this book has been to stress the importance of an evolutionary perspective on behavioural mechanisms. The same considerations should apply to the cognitive domain. Unfortunately comparatively little seems to have been written with regard to the circumstances which might favour the evolution of the sort of affectively linked biases in cognitive processing which we have been considering. This contrasts with the situation in perceptual processing (see Dixon 1972). Early work on recognition thresholds for emotionally laden material was often contradictory: negative material in particular sometimes seemed to produce higher thresholds — so-called perceptual defence — and sometimes lower thresholds. There were of course problems of response bias, but there were also questions of great theoretical importance. Whereas at one level efficient coping might be enhanced by operating a perceptual bias against the recognition of 'upsetting' material, at another level an animal in the wild is not well equipped for survival if it compromises perceptual efficiency in detecting warning stimuli of potentially life-threatening events. We would expect therefore that perceptual processing might well relate in a complex manner to the hedonic quality of stimuli presented. We know that people are capable of responding (at least autonomically) to words previously associated with shock, even though they are not consciously recognized (Forster and Govier 1978). We know also that anxiety has a disruptive effect on many aspects of cognitive processing (see chapter 8). It would seem sensible then that the organism should be capable of 'subconsciously' monitoring its environment for potential threats, but protects its processing systems from unnecessarily frequent impairment or overload by fixing a high threshold for affect-inducing recognition.

Selective retrieval in normal mood operates as we have seen in such a way as to favour positive items, that is, in mood congruence terms normal mood is to be seen as positively valenced. This may, indeed, normally favour efficient day-to-day coping. We might however speculate for the reasons given above that such mood congruence will not necessarily be as evident when considering perceptual phenomena.

It is interesting that using lexical decision tasks, which do not demand specific recognition of a word but only a decision that a stimulus is a word rather than a non-word, mood congruence for pleasant versus unpleasant material is a more evanescent phenomenon than in memory tasks. Findings are generally negative (Clark *et al.* 1983; MacLeod *et al.* 1987). Bray (1984) reports some evidence suggesting faster access for pleasant over unpleasant words in normal mood subjects, but later work suggests such differences may be small taken against the general speedier access for both pleasant and unpleasant words compared to neutral ones.

This speculative note is a suitable place to conclude this particular section, with the trite but accurate assessment that more work needs to be done.

THE CONSTRUCTION OF EMOTION

'To experience an emotion people must comprehend that their well-being is implicated in a transaction for better or worse' (Lazarus 1984). For Lazarus and other thoroughgoing cognitive theorists, it is clear that what they choose to call emotion depends on the individual's constructing that emotion out of an appraisal of the self in relation to the immediate environmental context. To quote Lazarus again: 'cognition of meaning' is a necessary pre-condition of emotion. Perhaps it is, but 'cognition of meaning' is not the easiest of concepts to pin down when it comes to testing Lazarus' proposition, if indeed it is meant to be testable. But rather than cover old ground, let us examine the essence of Lazarus' case, but less dogmatically with regard to what is and what is not an emotion.

151

With respect to emotional words, we are required to learn what linguistic philosophers might call a 'context of utterance' for such words. The social context then in a sense defines the emotion more than any associated bodily activities or inner feelings. Thus, attributing pride, shame, joy, 'the blues', to myself or others is merely part of what Wittgenstein showed to be a necessarily public 'language-game'. The essence of a particular emotion is not private feeling but public rule-following. Now this is not to be confused with a denial that inner feelings matter at all. We may imagine that a person with certain neurological damage may indicate that the intensity of his emotional feelings has diminished as a result of injury. What we cannot do, however, is to chase a defining feature through an inner feeling associated with a particular emotion X as opposed to a particular emotion Y. It would be as meaningless an exercise as ruminating over whether your sensation of 'red' differs from mine: the meaning of the word 'red' depends on public rules of reference, not on inner sensations. There is no mileage in 'private languages' to refer to sensations. In this sense Lazarus is correct to link cognition of meaning to emotion.

The 'constructivist' view which Lazarus espouses is however often lost in an over-concern with the individual's appraisals and cognitions. Harré (1983) succeeds succinctly in getting the linguistic point across by the simple device of describing historically how a specific 'emotion' can become extinct over the centuries as the context (social, religious, etc.) for its expression becomes irrelevant. Equally we could point to cross-cultural evidence that certain societies have specific words for 'states' which we certainly would want to call 'emotions' but which, by their contextual requirements, are seen to have no real parallels in our society. In a sense then, questions such as 'how many emotions are there?' are literally without meaning. On this view, emotions are social constructions which serve and bend to the needs of the linguistic community that uses words to label them. Every text which deals with the Sapir-Whorfe hypothesis concerning language and thought is inclined to mention the fact that Eskimos have several words for snow. In this post-Wittgensteinian age, emotion is as snow, and its taxonomy likewise has to do with utility and custom, not with some naïve realism as to what truly exists out there, or even more fallaciously in the case of emotion: 'in there'. But before language, what? And what of babes and savages?

If cognition is taken as a precondition of emotion, then emotional development must follow rather than precede cognitive development. As Leventhal (1979) points out, there is a contradiction here: a baby will have to learn about fearful, disgusting, angry, and joyous situations before it can truly be said to experience fear, disgust, anger, and joy: and yet how can the young infant come to know that situations have a certain emotional quality unless he or she first experiences the emotion in some sort of raw form? The idea that the child could first learn the emotional labelling of situations via imitation loses any credibility when we realize that young infants respond emotionally to different things from their purported parental models, and anyway, blind infants develop emotional responses to objects largely in the same way as sighted children. Finally developmental studies of emotion beginning with Bridges (1932) suggest a maturational pattern for the emergence of emotional behaviour which is at least partially independent of cognitive experience. Leventhal's conclusion that the development of emotional labels and concepts emerges out of basic or primary emotional experiences seems entirely warranted.

Note that the points we have just made are particularly forceful against the Schachterian type of theory which sees cognition as giving specificity to an otherwise undifferentiated state of arousal. If we are looking for some form of bodily feedback which could meet the requirement of specificity for different primary emotions, then the obvious focus is suggested by the work of Ekman and others, reported earlier, which demonstrates cross-cultural universality in the facial expression of at least certain primary emotions.

Theorists such as Leventhal, Izard, and Tomkins all place importance (though to differing degrees) on the role of feedback from the facial motor system in determining distinctive emotional states. The idea that such feedback may play at least some role has great plausibility, if only because of the findings with regard to universality of facial expression. The path from plausibility to proof however is a difficult one. Typical experiments have involved getting subjects to contract the facial musculature in ways such as to mimic emotional expressions. Subjects are then exposed to emotion eliciting material such as funny or sad films. Depending on whether the adopted facial expressions are congruent or incongruent with the exposure condition, it is reported that emotional states can be blocked or enhanced. Unfortunately all such studies illustrate 'demand characteristics' writ large. Although subjects are not told that the muscular manipulations mimic emotional expressions, it is hard to avoid the conclusion that subjects would work this out for themselves. Another problem which makes this aspect of emotion theory difficult to test is that voluntary and involuntary distinctions seem to be of crucial importance in determining the nature of experimental effects. Thus it may be that facial feedback normally does help determine the quality of a felt emotion, but only so long as attention is not voluntarily directed towards such feedback. Interestingly there is evidence, especially with regard to negative affective states, that voluntary concentration on physical aspects of the state actually reduces felt aversiveness. Thus behaviour therapists may well ask their clients to concentrate on their fear rather than a frightening situation, in the belief that something like 'fear of fear' can be diminished (see Evans 1972; and also T.S. Eliot's 'East Coker'). Equally, deliberate stuttering can be a beneficial therapy to inhibit involuntary and possibly emotionally induced stuttering. It is also hard to produce anything resembling the true feeling of being tickled simply by consciously and deliberately producing the physical stimulation. A final example: trying to blush is often a successful inhibitor of natural blushing. Largely for these reasons, eclectic models of emotion, such as that put forward by Leventhal (1979), would tend to see facial feedback as a pre-attentive check in the complex process of perceiving one's emotional state.

CONCLUSIONS

Here we must draw to a close. In the space available we have not even attempted to outline all of the very many theories of emotion that have been put forward by psychologists in recent times. There are specific texts which are more suited to that aim (see Strongman 1987). What we have tried to give the reader is the flavour of debate in what even psychologists themselves recognize as a messy and conceptually confusing area. Lord Rosebery, commenting on some piece of income tax legislation towards the turn of the century, is reputed to have said 'We're all socialists now.' Within psychology we have had two major so-called revolutions this century and both have left legacies of broad agreement on certain points of procedure and interpretation of findings within our discipline. To this extent it is true that we are all behaviourists now, and we are all cognitivists now. For that reason I think there is something wrong when I hear from some among my colleagues words to the effect that 'affect and emotion are going to be the big issues in cognitive psychology in the immediate future'. I see what they mean, but cognitive psychology has won all the battles it is ever going to win by fighting under a separate banner. As a defined area of psychology it is time it was disbanded. It is not for something called cognitive psychology to embrace motivational and emotional phenomena, rather the area of motivation and emotion has embraced and will continue to embrace cognitive concepts, as and when required, as long as they give rise to testable hypotheses.

References

Abramson, L.Y., Seligman, M.E.P., and Teasdale, J.D. (1978) 'Learned helplessness in humans: critique and reformulation', *Journal of Abnormal Psychology* 87: 49–74.

Alloy, L.B. and Abramson, L.Y (1979) 'Judgement of contingency in depressed and non-depressed students: sadder but wiser?', *Journal of Experimental Psychology: General* 108: 441–55.

Apter, M.J. (1982) *The Experience of Motivation*, London: Academic Press.

Atkinson, J.W. (1981) 'Studying personality in the context of an advanced motivational psychology', *American Psychologist* 36: 117–28.

—— and Litwin, G.H. (1960) 'Achievement motive and test anxiety conceived as a motive to approach success and to avoid failure', *Journal of Abnormal and Social Psychology* 60: 52–63.

Averill, J.R., O'Brien, L., and DeWitt, G.W. (1977) 'The influence of response effectiveness on the preference for warning and on psycho-physiological stress reactions', *Journal of Personality* 45: 395–418.

Ax, A.F. (1953) 'The physiological differentiation between fear and anger in humans', *Psychosomatic Medicine* 15: 433–42.

Badia, P., Harsh, J., and Abbott, B. (1979) 'Choosing between predictable and unpredictable shock conditions: data and theory', *Psychological Bulletin* 86: 1107–31.

Barash, D. (1981) *Sociobiology: the whisperings within*, Glasgow: Collins.

Bard, P. and Mountcastle, V.B. (1948) 'Some forebrain mechanisms involved in the expression of rage with special reference to suppression of angry behaviour', *Research publications of the Association of Nervous and Mental Disease* 27: 362–404.

Baron, R.A., Byrne, D., and Griffitt, W. (1974) *Social Psychology: understanding human interaction*, Boston: Allyn & Bacon.

Beck, A.T. (1974) 'The development of depression: a cognitive model', in R.J. Friedman and M.M. Katz (eds.) *The Psychology of Depression*, Washington: Winston.

Berlyne, D.E. (1960) *Conflict, Arousal, and Curiosity*, New York. McGraw-Hill.

—— (1967) 'Arousal and reinforcement', in D. Levine (ed) *Nebraska Symposium on Motivation (15)*, Lincoln: University of Nebraska Press.

Blaney, P. (1986) 'Affect and memory: a review', *Psychological Bulletin* 99, 2: 229–46.

Blundell, J. (1975) *Physiological Psychology*, London: Methuen.

Booth, D.A. (1981) 'The physiology of appetite', *British Medical Bulletin* 37: 135–40.

Bower, G.H. (1981) 'Mood and memory', *American Psychologist* 36: 129–48.

—— , McLean, J., and Meacham, J. (1966) 'The value of knowing when reinforcement is due', *Journal of Comparative and Physiological Psychology* 62: 184–92.

Boyd, T.L. and Levis, D.J. (1983) 'Exposure is a necessary condition for fear reduction: a reply to DeSilva & Rachman', *Behaviour Research and Therapy* 21: 143–9.

Brady, J.V. (1958) 'Ulcers in "executive make-up" ', *Scientific American* 199, 4: 95–100.

Bray, D. (1984) 'Influence of hedonic tone on lexical decisions', *Current Psychological Research and Reviews* 3: 63–9.

Brener, J. (1983) 'Visceral perception', in J. Beatty and H. Legewie (eds) *Biofeedback and Behavior*, New York: Plenum Press.

Bridges, K.M.B. (1932) 'Emotional development in early infancy', *Child Development* 3: 324–41.

Broadbent, D.E. (1971) *Decision and Stress*, London: Academic Press.

—— and Gregory, M. (1965) 'Effects of noise and of signal rate upon vigilance analysed by means of decision theory', *Human Factors* 7: 155–62.

Bugelski, B.R. (1938) 'Extinction with and without sub-goal reinforcement', *Journal of Comparative Psychology* 26: 121–33.

Byrne, D. and DeNinno, J.A. (1974) 'Response to erotic movies as a function of contextual effects', unpublished manuscript, Purdue University.

Cannon, W.B., Lewis, J.T., and Britton, S.W. (1927) 'The dispensability of the sympathetic division of the autonomic nervous system', *Boston Medical Surgical Journal* 197: 514–15.

Carroll, D., Turner, J.R., Lee, H.J., and Stephenson, J. (1984) 'Temporal consistency of individual differences in cardiac response to a video game', *Biological Psychology* 19: 81–93.

Clark, D.M., Teasdale, J.D., Broadbent, D.E., and Martin, M. (1983) 'Effect of mood on lexical decisions', *Bulletin of the Psychonomic Society* 21: 175–8.

Coons, E.E., Levak, M., and Miller, N.E. (1965) 'Lateral hypothalamus: learning of food seeking response motivated by electrical stimulation', *Science* 150: 1320–1.

Cooper, C.L. (ed.) (1983) *Stress Research: issues for the eighties*, London: Wiley.

Corcoran, D.W.J. (1963) 'Doubling the rate of signal presentation in a vigilance task during sleep deprivation', *Journal of Applied Psychology* 47: 412–15.

Covington, M.O. and Omelich, C.L. (1979) 'Are causal attributions causal? A path analysis of the cognitive model of achievement motivation', *Journal of Personality and Social Psychology* 37: 1487–504.

Cox, T. (1979) *Stress*, London: Macmillan.

Cromwell, R.L., Butterfield, E.C., Brayfield, F.M., and Curry, J.J. (1977) *Acute Myocardial Infarction: reaction and recovery*, St Louis, Mo: Mosby.

Dawkins, R. (1976) *The Selfish Gene*, Oxford: Oxford University Press.

Deci, E.L. (1975) *Intrinsic Motivation*, New York: Plenum.

Dement, W.C. (1960) 'The effect of dream deprivation', *Science* 131: 1705–7.

Dixon, N.F. (1972) *Subliminal Perception: the nature of a controversy*, London: McGraw-Hill.

—— (1976) *On the Psychology of Military Incompetence*, London: Jonathan Cape.

Duffy, E. (1957) 'The psychological significance of the concept of arousal or activation', *The Psychological Review* 64: 265–75.

Eccles, J. (1983) 'Expectancies, values and academic behaviors', in

J. Spence (ed.) *Achievement and Achievement Motives*, San Francisco: Freeman.

Egger, M.D. and Miller, N.E. (1962) 'Secondary reinforcement in rats as a function of information value and reliability of the stimulus', *Journal of Experimental Psychology* 64: 97–104.

Ekman, P. and Oster, H. (1982) 'Review and prospect', in P. Ekman (ed.) *Emotion in the Human Face*, 2nd ed., Cambridge: Cambridge University Press.

Ellis, A. (1980) 'Rational-emotive therapy and cognitive behavior therapy: similarities and differences', *Cognitive Therapy and Research* 4: 325–40.

Ellis, L. and Ames, M.A. (1987) 'Neurohormonal functioning and sexual orientation: a theory of homosexuality-heterosexuality', *Psychological Bulletin* 101: 233–58.

Erdman, G. and Janke, W. (1978) 'Interaction between physiological and cognitive determinants of emotions: experimental studies on Schachter's theory of emotions', *Biological Psychology* 6: 61–74.

Evans, I.M. (1972) 'A conditioning model of common neurotic patterns: fear of fear', *Psychotherapy, Theory Research and Practice* 9: 238–41.

Evans, P.D. (1983) 'Aggression and violence', in R. Bull, B. Bustin, P. Evans, and D. Gahagan, *Psychology for Police Officers*, London: Wiley.

—— , Phillips, K., and Fearn, J. (1984) 'On choosing to make aversive events predictable or unpredictable: some behavioural and psychophysiological findings', *British Journal of Psychology* 75: 377–91.

—— and Fearn, J. (1985) 'Type A behaviour pattern, choice of active coping strategy and cardiovascular activity in relation to threat of shock', *British Journal of Medical Psychology* 58: 95–9.

—— and Moran, P. (1987a) 'The Framingham type A Scale, vigilant coping and heart rate activity', *Journal of Behavioral Medicine* 10: 311–21.

—— and —— (1987b) 'Cardiovascular unwinding, type A behaviour pattern, and locus of control', *British Journal of Medical Psychology*, 60: 261–5.

Eysenck, H.J. (1967) *The Biological Basis of Personality*, Springfield, Ill.: Thomas.

—— (1981) 'General features of the model', in H.J. Eysenck (ed.) *A Model for Personality*, Berlin: Springer-Verlag.

—— and Eysenck, S.B.G. (1975) *Manual of the Eysenck Personality Questionnaire*, Sevenoaks: Hodder & Stoughton.

Eysenck, M.W. (1984) *A Handbook of Cognitive Psychology*, London: Laurence Erlbaum Associates.

Fantino, E. and Logan, A. (1979) *The Experimental Analysis of Behavior: a biological approach*, San Francisco: Freeman.

Fineman, S. (1977) 'The achievement motive construct and its measurement: where are we now?', *British Journal of Psychology* 68: 1–22.

Flood, J.F., Landry, D.W., Bennett, E.L., and Jarvik, M.E. (1981) 'Long-term memory disruption by inhibitors of protein synthesis and cytoplasmic flow', *Pharmacology, Biochemistry, and Behaviour* 15: 289–96.

Ford, C.S. and Beach, F.A. (1951) *Patterns of Sexual Behavior*, New York: Harper.

Forster, P.M. and Govier, E. (1978) 'Discrimination without awareness?', *Quarterly Journal of Experimental Psychology* 30: 289–95.

Frankenhaeuser, M. (1980) 'Psychoneuroendocrine approaches to the study of stressful person-environment transactions', in H. Selye (ed.) *Guide to Stress Research*, vol. 1, New York: Van Nostrand Reinhold.

French, E.G. and Thomas, F. (1958) 'The relation of achievement motivation to problem-solving effectiveness', *Journal of Abnormal and Social Psychology* 56: 45–8.

Freud, S. (1954) *The Interpretation of Dreams* (originally published 1900), English translation: London: Allen & Unwin.

Fromm, E. (1977) *The Anatomy of Human Destructiveness*, Harmondsworth: Penguin Books.

Gale, A. (1981) 'EEG studies of extraversion-introversion: What's the next step?', in R. Lynn (ed.) *Dimensions of Personality: papers in honour of H.J. Eysenck*, Oxford: Pergamon.

Garcia, J. and Koelling, R.A. (1966) 'Relation of cue to consequences in avoidance learning', *Psychonomic Science* 4: 123–4.

—— and Rusiniak, K.W. (1980) 'What the nose learns from the mouth', in D. Muller-Schwarze and R.M. Silverstein (eds) *Chemical Signals*, New York: Plenum Press.

Glass, D.C. (1977) *Behavior Patterns, Stress, and Coronary Disease*, Hillsdale, New Jersey: Erlbaum.

Goldfried, M.R. and Davison, G.C. (1976) *Clinical Behavior Therapy*, New York: Holt Rinehart & Winston.

Gray, J. (1971) *The Psychology of Fear and Stress*, London: Weidenfeld & Nicolson.

—— and Smith, P.T. (1969) in: R.M. Gilbert and N.J. Sutherland (eds) *Animal Discrimination Learning*, London: Academic Press.

Harré, R. (1983) *Personal Being*, Oxford: Blackwell.

Hebb, D.O. (1955) 'Drives and the conceptual nervous system', *Psychological Review* 62: 243–54.

—— (1966) *A Textbook of Psychology*, 2nd ed., Philadelphia: Saunders.

Helmreich, R.L., Spence, J.T., Beane, W.E., Lucker, G.W., and Matthews, K.A. (1980) 'Making it in academic psychology: demographic and personality correlates of attainment', *Journal of Personality and Social Psychology* 39: 896–908.

Herman, C.P. and Polivy, J. (1980) 'Restrained eating', in A.B. Stunkard (ed.), *Obesity*, Philadelphia: Saunders.

Herzberg, F. (1966) *Work and the Nature of Man*, Cleveland: World.

Hirschmann, R.D. (1975) 'Cross-modal effects of anticipatory bogus heart rate feedback in a negative emotional context', *Journal of Personality and Social Psychology* 31: 13–19.

Hohmann, G.W. (1966) 'Some effects of spinal cord lesions on experienced emotional feelings', *Psychophysiology* 3: 143–56.

Holmes, T.H. and Rahe, R.H. (1967) 'The social readjustment rating scale', *Journal of Psychosomatic Research* 11: 213–18.

Horner, M. (1968) 'Sex differences in achievement motivation and performance in competitive and non-competitive situations', unpublished doctoral thesis, University of Michigan.

Humphreys, M.S., Revelle, W., Simon, L., and Gilliland, K. (1980) 'Individual differences in diurnal rhythms and multiple activation states: a reply to M.W. Eysenck & Follard', *Journal of Experimental Psychology: General* 108: 42–8.

Idzikowski, C. (1984) 'Sleep and memory', *British Journal of Psychology* 75: 439–49.

Izard, C.E. (1984) 'Emotion-cognition relationships and human development', in C.E. Izard, J. Kagan, and R.B. Zajonc (eds) *Emotions, Cognition, and Behavior*, New York: Cambridge University Press.

Janis, I.L. (1958) *Psychological Stress*, New York: Wiley.

Jenkins, J.G. and Dallenbach, K.M. (1924) 'Oblivescence during sleep and waking', *American Journal of Psychology* 35: 605–12.

Johnson, J.E. and Leventhal, H. (1974) 'Effects of accurate expectations and behavioral instructions on reactions during a noxious medical examination', *Journal of Personality and Social Psychology* 29: 710–18.

—— , Petzel, T.P., Hartney, L.M., and Morgan, L.M. (1983) 'Recall and importance ratings of completed and uncompleted tasks as a function of depression', *Cognitive Therapy and Research* 7: 51–6.

Jouvet, M. (1967) 'The sleeping brain', *Science Journal*, May, special issue: 133–48.

Katz, R. and Wykes, T. (1985) 'The psychological difference between temporally predictable and unpredictable stressful events: evidence for information control theories', *Journal of Personality and Social Psychology* 48: 781–90.

Kendler, H.H. (1945) 'Drive interaction: learning as a function of the simultaneous presence of the hunger and thirst drives', *Journal of Experimental Psychology* 35: 96–109.

Kinsey, A.C., Pomeroy, W.B., and Martin, C.E. (1948) *Sexual Behavior in the Human Male*, Philadelphia: Saunders.

Kinsey, A.C., Pomeroy, W.B., Martin, C.E., and Gebhard, P.H. (1953) *Sexual Behavior in the Human Female*, Philadelphia: Saunders.

Lacey, J.I. (1967) 'Somatic response patterning and stress: some revisions of activation theory', in M.H. Appley and R. Trumble eds) *Psychological Stress*, New York: Appleton-Century-Crofts.

Lange, C. (1885) original monograph translated in: K. Dunlap (1967) (ed.) *The Emotions*, New York: Hafner.

Lazarus, R.S. (1974) 'Psychological stress and coping in adaptation and illness', *International Journal of Psychiatry in Medicine* 5: 321–33.

—— (1984) 'On the primacy of cognition', *American Psychologist* 39, 2: 124–9.

Lepper, M.R. and Greene, D. (1978) *The Hidden Costs of Reward: new perspectives on the psychology of human motivation*, New Jersey: Lawrence Erlbaum.

Leventhal, H. (1979) 'A perceptual-motor processing model of emotion', in P. Pliner, K.R. Blankstein, and I.M. Spigel (eds) *Perception of Emotion in Self and Others*, New York: Plenum.

Light, K.C. and Obrist, P.A. (1983) 'Task difficulty, heart rate reactivity, and cardiovascular responses to an appetitive reaction time task', *Psychophysiology* 20: 301–12.

Lindsley, D.B. (1957) 'Psychophysiology and motivation', in M.R. Jones (ed.) *Nebraska Symposium on Motivation* (5), Lincoln: University of Nebraska Press.

—— (1961) 'Common factors in sensory deprivation, sensory distortion and sensory overload', in P. Solomon, P.E. Kubzansky, P.H. Leiderman,

160

J.H. Mendelson, R. Trumbull, and D. Wexler (eds) *Sensory Deprivation*, Cambridge, Mass: Harvard University Press.

Littman, R.A., and Manning, H.M. (1954) 'A methodological study of cigarette brand discrimination', *Journal of Applied Psychology* 38: 185–90.

Lowe, J. and Carroll, D. (1985) 'The effects of spinal injury on the intensity of emotional experience', *British Journal of Clinical Psychology* 24: 135–6.

Lowell, E.L. (1952) 'The effect of need for achievement on learning and speed of performance', *Journal of Psychology* 33: 31–40.

Maccoby, E.E. and Jacklin, C.N. (1974) *The Psychology of Sex Differences*, Stanford: Stanford University Press.

MacLean, P.D. (1949) 'Psychosomatic disease and the visceral brain: recent developments bearing on the Papez theory of emotion', *Psychosomatic Medicine* 11: 338–53.

MacLeod, C., Tata, P., and Mathews, A. (1987) 'Perception of emotionally valenced information in depression', *British Journal of Clinical Psychology* 26: 67–8.

Malone, C. (1960) 'Fear of failure in unrealistic vocational aspirations', *Journal of Abnormal and Social Psychology* 60: 253–61.

Marsh, P. (1982) 'Rhetorics of violence', in P. Marsh and A. Campbell (eds) *Aggression and Violence*, Oxford: Blackwell.

Maslow, A.H. (1954) *Motivation and Personality*, New York: Harper.

Mason, J.W. (1971) 'A re-evaluation of the concept of non-specificity in stress research', *Journal of Psychiatric Research* 8: 323–33.

Matthews, G. (1985) 'The effects of extraversion and arousal on intelligence test performance', *British Journal of Psychology* 76: 479–93.

Matthews, K.A. (1982) 'Psychological perspectives on the Type A behavior pattern', *Psychological Bulletin* 91: 293–323.

McClelland, D.C., Atikinson, J.W., Clark, R.W., and Lowell, E.L. (1953) *The Achievement Motive*, New York: Appleton-Century-Crofts.

Meller, R. (1982) 'Aggression in primate social groups: hormonal correlates', in P. Marsh and A. Campbell (eds) *Aggression and Violence*, Oxford: Blackwell.

Meryman, J.J. (1952) 'Magnitude of the startle response as a function of hunger and fear', unpublished doctoral thesis, University of Iowa.

Michelmore, S. (1964) *Sex*, London: Eyre & Spottiswoode.

Milgram, S. (1963) 'Behavioral study of obedience', *Journal of Abnormal and Social Psychology* 67: 371–8.

Miller, N.E., Bailey, C.J., and Stevenson, J.A.F. (1950) 'Decreased "hunger" but increased food intake resulting from hypothalamic lesions', *Science* 112: 256–9.

Miller, S.M. (1979a) 'Coping with impending stress: psychophysiological and cognitive correlates of choice', *Psychophysiology* 16: 572–81.

—— (1979b) 'Controllability and human stress: method, evidence and theory', *Behaviour Research and Therapy* 17: 287–304.

——, and Mangan, C.E. (1983) 'Interacting effects of information and coping style in adapting to gynaecologic stress: should the doctor tell all?' *Journal of Personality and Social Psychology* 45: 223–36.

Mineka, S. (1979) 'The role of fear in theories of avoidance learning, flooding, and extinction', *Psychological Bulletin* 86: 985–1010.

Mischel, W. (1961) 'Delay of gratification, need for achievement, and acquiescence in another culture', *Journal of Abnormal and Social Psychology* 62: 543–52.

Morgan, M. (1982) 'Theoretical interpretations of over-justification effects', *Current Psychology Reviews* 2, 2: 213–29.

Moruzzi, G. (1964) 'Reticular influences in the EEG', *Electroencephalogy and Clinical Neurophysiology* 16: 2–17.

—— , and Magoun, H.W. (1949) 'Brain stem reticular formation and activation of the EEG', *EEG Clinical Neurophysiology* 1: 455–73.

Mulville, F. (1986) 'The unseen enemy', *Yachting Monthly* 147, no. 958.

Murgatroyd, S., Rushton, C., Apter, M.J., and Ray, C. (1978) 'The development of the telic dominance scale', *Journal of Personality Assessment* 42: 519–28.

Nisbett, R.E. (1972) 'Hunger, obesity, and the ventromedial hypothalamus', *Psychological Review* 79: 433–53.

Olds, J. (1956) 'Pleasure centers in the brain', *Scientific American* 195: 105–16.

Oswald, I. (1966) *Sleep*, Harmondsworth: Penguin Books.

Papez, J.W. (1937) 'A proposed mechanism of emotion', *Archives of Neurological Psychiatry* 38: 725–43.

Peele, S. and Brodsky, A. (1977) *Love and Addiction*, London: Sphere.

Pillard, R.C., Poumadere, J., and Carretta, R.A. (1982) 'A family study of sexual orientation', *Archives of Sexual Behavior* 11: 511–20.

Power, M.J. and Champion, L.A. (1986) 'Cognitive approaches to depression: a theoretical critique', *British Journal of Clinical Psychology* 25: 201–13.

Powley, T.L. (1977) 'The ventromedial hypothalamic syndrome, satiety, and a cephalic phase hypothesis', *Psychological Review* 84: 89–126.

Quattrone, G.A. (1985) 'On the congruity between internal states and action', *Psychological Bulletin* 98: 3–40.

Rachlin, H. (1976) *Behavior and Learning*, Oxford: Freeman.

Ranieri, D.J. and Zeiss, A.M. (1984) 'Induction of depressed mood: a test of opponent-process theory', *Journal of Personality and Social Psychology* 47: 1413–22.

Redgrave, P. and Dean, P. (1981) 'Intracranial self-stimulation', *British Medical Bulletin* 37: 141–6.

Revelle, W., Amaral, P., and Turriff, S. (1976) 'Introversion/extraversion, time stress and caffeine: the effect on verbal performance', *Science* 192: 149–50.

Revelle, W., Humphreys, M.S., Simon, L., and Gilliland, K. (1980) 'The interactive effect of personality, time of day, and caffeine: a test of the arousal model', *Journal of Experimental Psychology: General* 109: 1–31.

Roberts, W.W. (1958) 'Both rewarding and punishing effects from stimulation of posterior hypothalamus of cats with same electrode of same intensity', *Journal of Comparative Physiology and Psychology* 51: 400–7.

Rodin, J. (1981) 'Current status of the internal-external hypothesis for obesity: what went wrong?', *American Psychologist* 36: 361–72.

—— , Slochower, J., and Fleming, B. (1977) 'Effects of degree of obesity, age of onset and weight loss on responsiveness to sensory and external stimuli', *Journal of Comparative and Physiological Psychology* 91: 586–97.

Rolls, E.T. (1981) 'Central nervous system mechanisms related to feeding and appetite', *British Medical Bulletin* 37: 131–4.

Rotter, J.B. (1966) 'Generalized expectancies for internal versus external locus of control of reinforcement', *Psychological Monographs* 80: 1–28.

Ruderman, A.J. (1986) 'Dietary restraint: a theoretical and empirical review', *Psychological Bulletin* 99: 247–62.

Runge, T.E. (1980) 'Work, leisure and personality: a multivariate approach to life satisfaction', doctoral thesis, University of Texas, Austin.

Rycroft, C. (1966) 'Introduction: causes and meaning', in C. Rycroft (ed.) *Psychoanalysis Observed*, London: Constable.

Savin-Williams, R.C. (1977) 'Dominance in a human adolescent group', *Animal Behaviour* 25: 400–6.

Schachter, S. (1971) 'Some extraordinary facts about obese humans and rats', *American Psychologist* 26: 129–44.

—— , and Singer, J.E. (1962) 'Cognitive, social and physiological determinants of emotional state', *Psychological Review* 69: 379–99.

Schmidt, G. and Schafer, S. (1973) 'Responses to reading erotic stories: male-female differences', *Archives of Sexual Behavior* 2: 181–99.

Schuster, R.H. (1969) 'A functional analysis of conditioned reinforcement', in D.P. Hendry (ed.) *Conditioned Reinforcement*, Homewood, Illinois: The Dorsey Press.

Seamon, J.J., Brody, N., and Kauff, D.M. (1983) 'Affective discrimination of stimuli that are not recognized: effects of shadowing, masking, and cerebral laterality', *Journal of Experimental Psychology, Learning, Memory and Cognition* 9: 544–55.

Selye, H. (1956) *The Stress of Life*, New York: McGraw-Hill.

Sigusch, V., Schmidt, G., Reinfeld, A., and Wiedermann-Sutor, I. (1970) 'Psychosexual stimulation: sex differences', *Journal of Sex Research* 6: 10–24.

Smith, B.D. (1983) 'Extraversion and electrodermal activity: arousability and the inverted U', *Personality and Individual Differences* 4: 411–19.

Solomon, R.L. (1980) 'The opponent-process theory of acquired motivation: the costs of pleasure and the benefits of pain', *American Psychologist* 35: 691–712.

Spence, J.T. and Spence, K.W. (1966) 'The motivational components of manifest anxiety: drive and drive stimuli', in C.D. Spielberger (ed.) *Anxiety and Behavior*, London: Academic Press.

—— ., and Helmreich, R.L. (1983) 'Achievement-related motives and behavior', in J.T. Spence (ed.) *Achievement and Achievement Motives: psychological and sociological approaches*, San Francisco: Freeman.

Starr, M.D. (1978) 'An opponent-process theory of motivation, VI. Time and intensity variables in the development of separation-induced distress calling in ducklings', *Journal of Experimental Psychology: Animal behaviour processes* 4: 338–55.

Stellar, E. (1954) 'The physiology of motivation', *Psychological Review* 61: 5–22.

Strongman, K.T. (1987) *The Psychology of Emotion*, 3rd ed. London: Wiley.

Taylor, A., Sluckin, W., Davies, D.R., Reason, J.T., Thomson, R., and Colman, A.M. (1982) *Introducing Psychology*, 2nd ed. Harmondsworth: Penguin Books.

Thompson, S.C. (1981) 'Will it hurt less if I can control it? A complex answer to a simple question', *Psychological Bulletin* 90: 89–101.

Tilley, A.J. (1981) 'Retention over a period of REM or non-REM sleep', *British Journal of Psychology* 72: 241–8.

—— , and Empson, J.A.C. (1978) 'REM sleep and memory consolidation', *Biological Psychology* 6: 293–300.

Tomkins, S.S. (1982) 'Affect theory', in P. Ekman (ed.) *Emotion in the Human Face*, 2nd ed. Cambridge: Cambridge University Press.

Valins, S. and Ray, A.A. (1967) 'Effects of cognitive dissonance on avoidance behaviour', *Journal of Personality and Social Psychology* 7: 345–50.

Van Toller, C. (1979) *The Nervous Body*, London: Wiley.

Vogel, G.W. (1975) 'A review of REM sleep deprivation', *Archives of General Psychiatry* 32: 749–61.

Walter, J.D. (1981) 'Police in the middle: a study of small city police intervention in domestic disputes', *Journal of Police Science and Administration* 9: 243–60.

Weinberg, S. (1975) *Society and the Healthy Homosexual*, Gerrards Cross, Buckinghamshire: Colin Smythe.

Weiner, B. (1972) *Theories of Motivation: from mechanism to cognition*, Chicago: Markham.

—— , Heckhauzen, H., Meyer, W.U., and Cook, R.E. (1972) 'Causal attributions and achievement activation: a conceptual analysis of effort and reanalysis of locus of control', *Journal of Personality and Social Psychology* 21: 239–51.

Weiss, J.M. (1977) 'Psychological and behavioural influences on gastrointestinal lesions in animal models', in J.D. Maser and M.E.P. Seligman (eds) *Psychopathology: experimental models*, San Francisco: Freeman.

Wilkinson, R.T. (1963) 'Interaction of noise with knowledge of results and sleep deprivation', *Journal of Experimental Psychology* 66: 332–7.

Wilson, E.O. (1975) *Sociobiology: the new synthesis*, Cambridge, Mass: Harvard University Press.

Wolfe, J.B. (1936) 'Effectiveness of token rewards for chimps', *Comparative Psychology Monographs* 12, 60.

Wundt, W.M. (1893) *Grundzuge der physiologischen psychologie*, Leipzig: Engleman.

Yerkes, R.M. and Dodson, J.D. (1908) 'The relation of strength of stimulus to rapidity of habit formation', *Journal of Comparative and Neurological Psychology* 18: 459–82.

Zajonc, R.B. (1984) 'On the primacy of affect', *American Psychologist* 39, 2: 117–23.

Zillman, D. (1979) *Hostility and Aggression*, New Jersey: Erlbaum.

Zimbardo, P. (1972) 'Pathology of imprisonment', *Trans-Action* 9: 4–8.

Zuckerman, M. (1979) *Sensation Seeking: beyond the optimal level of arousal*, New Jersey: Laurence Erlbaum Associates.

Index

paired associate learning, 95
parasympathetic system, *see*
    autonomic nervous system
paratelic state, *see*
    metamotivation states
Pavlovian conditioning, 60, 69,
    93
perceptual processing, 150
persistence, 115, 120
pornography, 32, 33
predictability, 73, 76
promiscuity, 31-2
Proust, M., 27
psychoanalysis, 3, 5, 27, 88
psychopathy, 107
punishment, and aggression,
    51-2; neurophysiology of,
    63, 104

REM sleep, 19, 21, 24-7
reticular activating system, 20,
    90, 94
reversals, 110-11
risk-taking, 104, 106

sadism, 45, 49
safety-signal hypothesis, 73-6
secondary reinforcers, 69-74,
    89
sensation-seeking, 45, 105-7
sex and, 'drive', 29-30;
    orientation, 34-9;
    responsivity, 30-3; variation,
    33-4
sex differences, in aggression,
    40, 42; in achievement,
    124-8; in sensation-seeking,
    107; in sexual responsivity,
    30-3
sleep, and EEG, 18-20; and
    memory consolidation, 23-4;
    brain control mechanisms,

19-21; deprivation, 22-5, 91,
    92, 96, 100; need for, 21-2
sociobiology, 74
social influence, *see*
    conformity and obedience
survival needs, 8,
sympathetic system, *see*
    autonomic nervous system

taste conditioning, 14, 140
telic state, *see* metamotivational
    states
temperature regulation, 8
testosterone; *see also* hormones,
    37, 43
Thanatos, 88
Thematic Apperception Test,
    (TAT), 114-15
token exchange, 132
Type A behaviour, 76, 78, 81

ulcers, 81-2
unconscious (also subconscious)
    processes, 26, 27, 28, 140,
    150-1

values, *see also*
    expectancy-value theory,
    127-8
vigilance, *see also* coping,
    76-8, 92, 96
violence, *see also* aggression;
    and alcohol, 47; media
    portrayal, 46; rhetorics of, 44

William of Occam, 96
Wittgenstein, L., 137, 152
work, motivation at, 129-30;
    orientation, 126

Yerkes-Dodson Law, 87, 90, 99

Zeigarnik effect, 116, 148